I0481144

MIQUEL VIDAL

Cryptocurrency Trading Guide for Beginners

Learn how to build a simple and effective trading strategy to start investing in Bitcoin and other cryptocurrencies

Contents

III   Building Your Trading Strategy

I

Introduction

Chapter 1

Introduction

Do you want to become a millionaire in one day? Then this is not your book. I don't believe in any method that preaches that you can become a millionaire in one day.

Do you want to quit your 9 to 5 job and go live in a tropical paradise next month? Then this isn't a book for you either.

This is a book for people who have a job and want to start investing in cryptocurrencies – or 'trading' cryptocurrencies – without spending 8 hours a day. This is also a book for someone who has already tried it and realized that it is a very complicated world and needs a foundation to get started. Am I saying that you can't make a living from trading cryptocurrencies? Not at all, I'm just saying that you need to take baby steps. Before you learn to run, you have to learn to walk.

Statistics say that 95% of people who trade end up losing money sooner or later in the long run. 95%! I include myself in that 95%, and there's a good chance that if you've tried to trade someday, you have fallen into that large percentage of people as well. But why do the vast majority of people end up losing money? The answer to this question is simple. When it comes to money, people don't think with their rational brain, but with their emotional brain. And when money is involved, the emotional brain is dominated by two powerful emotions in all animals: fear and greed. I will try to explain this concept from a biological point of view very quickly.

The human brain is made up of layers that have evolved over millions of years from the first reptiles to today's mammals. Each layer is responsible for carrying out certain tasks. For example, modern mammals have a layer called the neocortex (the outer part of the brain), which in humans is highly developed and is responsible for making rational decisions, making plans, and designing short and long term strategies.

Below the neocortex, we find another layer that governs our more basic behavior, emotions, and links them to events in our lives. This is the limbic system.

And finally, at the base of our brain, we can find the reptilian brain, the oldest layer of our brain that takes care of the most basic functions. Here, the instincts that have enabled our ancestors to survive for millions of years are burned into our genetic code. And among these instincts are fear and greed.

In a normal situation, we use our neocortex to think. It is clear to all of us that we should use this layer when deciding whether to buy or sell an asset, be it a stock, a cryptocurrency, or shoes. But the reality is entirely different. The reptilian brain is very basic, but it is also much faster than the neocortex. We use it to make quick, life-or-death decisions, completely unconscious choices. For example, our brain is designed so that if it sees any danger, like a tiger hiding behind some bushes in the jungle, it will make you run in the opposite direction as fast as possible. To make you do this, the reptilian brain releases a series of chemical compounds. These compounds act immediately on your body, making it much better prepared to perform physical actions such as running at maximum speed or fighting with all your strength to survive. One of these compounds is adrenaline and has a side effect: it blocks the neocortex.

Well, it seems that the human brain, most of the time, treats money as an essential and necessary good for life. Therefore, many of the decisions involving money are not taken entirely by our neocortex but by our most basic brain. This not only happens to traders but also occurs when we make purchases of any product. Have you ever heard of compulsive buying? I am sure you have made some compulsive purchases in your life and probably very recently. Sellers and advertising agencies understand very well that to decide what to buy, we don't use the neocortex - the reason - but we use our most basic emotions. The more extreme the situation, the less we use our neocortex, and the more we use our reptilian brain.

But it turns out that the reptilian brain, ruled by the most basic emotions of fear and greed, is quite bad at making buying and selling decisions. In fact, it usually takes the opposite of the optimal decision. The reptilian brain, based on fear and greed, urges us to buy at the moment we should be thinking about selling, in times of high prices; this is our greed in action. And in moments of economic crisis when prices are falling, when we should be thinking about buying, our reptilian brain urges us to sell; this is fear in action. This means that many times we buy expensive, and many times we sell cheap creating a cycle from which it is hard to get out. And this is the simple reason why 95% of traders lose money. The reptilian brain blocks the neocortex.

The goal of this book is to help you create a simple step-by-step, long-term strategy for investing in cryptocurrencies so that you do not use your reptilian brain to make decisions. To do this, we simply have to define an investment strategy — also called a trading strategy — when we are relaxed and our neocortex is in command, and follow this strategy to the letter to avoid making decisions at the moment when our reptilian brain has taken over. You must create this strategy yourself so that it is adapted to your personality and your portfolio. In this book, I will show you how to design your basic strategy so that you can, over time, evolve and adapt it as you improve and gain experience.

This book is explicitly focused on cryptocurrencies, but the method for creating a trading strategy also works for stocks and other assets since the basic concepts are the same. This book is for people who do not want to spend the whole day buying and selling cryptocurrencies, so I will not explain day trading strategies in-depth. However, if your goal is to be a day trader, this book can give you the basics to achieve it in the future. If you still don't know what kind of trader you want to become, keep reading...

Chapter 2

Trader Types

Before you even think about creating a trading strategy, you should think about what kind of trading you want to do. Like everything in life, this is not 'black' or 'white'. Keep in mind that there are always grey areas. Let's see the basic types:

Day Trader. Day traders make very short buy and sell trades in time, which they call intraday trading. They don't leave open trades overnight and always keep an eye on their open trades. Their trades can last, from buying to selling, from a few minutes to a few hours. Their profit margins per trade are not very big, but they do a lot of trading a year, and that's where the profit accumulation comes from. Day traders benefit from highly volatile markets, as this allows them to increase the potential profit margin per trade in the short time available to them. They also need to operate markets with considerable liquidity. That means markets where enough people are buying and selling in the market to be able to quickly enter and exit their trades. Cryptocurrencies attract this type of traders because of their high volatility. This is probably the type of trading that made you interested in cryptocurrencies or any other kind of asset. The truth is that day trading is a type of trading that makes a lot of sense if you think about it. If you never leave your trades open when you are not watching, you can't have surprises like sudden and sharp price drops. These days you can find tons of self-proclaimed day traders on Youtube and other platforms. They proclaim the benefits of this lifestyle: "Leave your 9 to 5 job, trade for an hour a day and live wherever you want". Usually, these people offer some kind of training or classes, generally quite costly, and the reality is that many of them live off this income, from the people who pay for their classes. As I said in the introduction, I'm not saying that this lifestyle is not possible. It is totally doable. In fact, I know several day traders personally who lead that lifestyle, and that's why I don't recommend it to anyone who doesn't have a lot of trading experience. Day trading without having a good strategy and without controlling your reptilian brain is the fastest way to lose your money. In addition to that, day trading means being available, in front of the computer and completely focused during the high volatility moments of the market. But you don't know when those moments will come. If you're working, you probably won't be able to do day trading at the same time. For these reasons, this guide will not cover this type of trading. Also, I do not recommend anyone to start day trading without many years of experience in other types of trading.

Swing Trader. Swing Traders, unlike Day Traders, keep open trades for several days or even weeks. Swing Traders try to follow medium-term market trends and identify changes in these trends to place their buy and sell orders. Swing traders can base their trades on certain targets, for example, 15% profit for a possible 6% loss, or they can rely on technical indicators. We will talk about these indicators in much more detail in the third part of this book. This type of trading is also very popular. Many day traders are not pure day traders, but sometimes, and depending on the state of the market, they can hold longer-term trades, entering the realm of swing traders.

Investor. Investors make very long-term trades, from many months to several years. They try to buy at times of falling markets, when prices are low, and sell at times of market boom. If one day prices fall by 15%, investors are not affected as they think that 15% is insignificant in the long term. This type of trading is the closest to a passive income. However, I am not in favor of using the term 'passive' when talking about investment and much less in trading. Even long-term investors need to do something to take care of their assets. It is true that investors don't need to be trading every day or even watching their investments every day. Still, if they want to make a profit, they do need to spend time watching their investments and, above all, looking for opportunities. If you are going to take care of your money, there is no completely passive solution. You are always going to have to dedicate part of your time, whether you invest in cryptocurrencies, stocks — including dividends—, or real estate.

As I said before, these different types of traders are not exclusive. Day traders can, and typically do, multi-day trades. Swing traders can make very long-term trades, or also intraday trades. And investors can make shorter-term trades depending on the state of the market.

The truth is that engaging in one type of trading or another is going to depend very much on your personality, your stress and risk tolerance, and your personal situation and goals in life. I can't decide for you, but I can give you the basics so you can make an informed decision. The more you trade, the more likely you are to make a mistake, so day trading is the riskiest way, but the one that potentially allows you to take better advantage of small market movements. Investors assume less risk by taking advantage of long-term market trends. Still, they also have less potential profit, as they do not take advantage of smaller market movements. Swing traders are in the middle, accepting less risk than day traders, but more than investors. My recommendation is to start with longer trades. Learn to read the market movements at a higher level, and if you are interested in swing trading and day trading, gradually make shorter and more frequent trades. This book is aimed at people who have little experience and for people who don't want to spend all day (and night) trading the markets. For that reason, we will design together a strategy that would be halfway between an investor and a swing trader. In the cryptocurrency market, which is a market where prices can vary a lot in a short period of time, the goal will be to make a few trades per month. In this way, you can get started in the world of trading cryptocurrencies, learn the techniques, and above all, learn to control your reptilian brain without taking too much risk. After that, with time, if you want to move on to other types of trading, you will be able to do it safely. Remember, you have to walk before you can run.

II

Basic Concepts

In this part of the book, you are going to have a first contact with the world of cryptocurrencies. We will see what they are, how to analyze them, and I will show you a couple of handy tools that you can use in your day to day. At the end of this part, you will have built the foundation of your trading strategy for cryptocurrencies.

Chapter 3

Cryptocurrencies From Scratch

This book is focused on investment in cryptocurrencies, but you will find many concepts that can be applied to invest in any other type of asset. In this part of the book, I will make a basic introduction to cryptocurrencies. What they are, what technology they are based on, and why I think they are going to be so important in the future. If you are not very interested in how cryptocurrencies work or you have enough experience and knowledge about what cryptocurrencies are, you can jump to the third part of the book. But I would recommend you to read at least chapter 4. In chapter 4, I explain how to quickly analyze the ideas and solutions behind a particular cryptocurrency and how to identify the ones that have a solid foundation. That will also be the first step to build your cryptocurrency trading strategy.

History and Technology

You can find a lot of information, both written and in videos and documentaries about the history of cryptocurrencies on the Internet, blogs, television, Netflix, Youtube... Besides, this book is not only for computer programmers, so I will not extend much in this part, as it can be very technical.

The history of cryptocurrencies began with the birth of Bitcoin in 2009. Bitcoin was created during 2008, supposedly by a 'somebody' named Satoshi Nakamoto. There's a lot of speculation about whether Satoshi Nakamoto really exists, who he is, and what became of him (or them). Bitcoin is a computer program designed to run on different computers at the same time. This is called distributed processing. The Bitcoin code was released as open-source in 2009, so everyone can see it and use it.

Remember that in 2007-2008 there was a global financial crisis that led to the collapse of some large financial institutions. When these institutions started to fall, the governments of the world, to avoid a domino effect, started to rescue these institutions that were in danger. Central banks have the ability to 'print money', and they used it. Banks in general around the world were rightly blamed for causing the 2008 crisis. A significant number of countries in Europe had a relatively new common currency at that moment, the Euro, which was at that time just over 8 years old. These countries had lost the ability to devalue their currency independently. Some of them, like Spain, Italy, and Greece, found themselves in serious trouble due to economic weakness. In Europe, this triggered a new crisis from 2009 onwards, and today, in 2020, we are still feeling the effects. But this is another story...

The problem that emerged from the 2008 crisis caused by the banks is that people began to distrust these institutions, which had become incredibly rich until they ended up affecting the entire economy. But the banks, together with the central banks, still had control of the currency. Therefore, to perform any economic transaction using money, people had to use (and trust) the banks. And more importantly, to do any digital financial transaction without using physical money such as bills or coins, we needed to use an intermediary. To make a purchase, for example, with a credit or debit card, through the Internet or through a transfer, we needed three actors: the buyer, the seller, and this third entity, which is a financial institution, a bank. This third entity is important because it means that the buyer and the seller do not have to trust each other, they just need to trust this intermediary. This intermediary is an entity with a reputation and a government behind it that guarantees the validity of the money and the transactions. But during this crisis, the general public realized that the banks really only hold a very small fraction of the money that people deposit in them, and most of this money is used to give loans and mortgages. This in itself is not bad, but the problem comes when banks, blindly focused on making more and more profits every year, do not establish sufficient control and security to be somewhat sure that this borrowed money can be returned. This lack of control is precisely what triggered the crisis in 2008. Moreover, since they only hold a very small fraction of the money, if a significant percentage of people decided to take their money out of the banks at the same time because they do not believe their money is safe in the bank, the banks would not have enough liquidity to do so. This became very clear during the 2008 crisis and generated a state of distrust in these financial institutions.

In addition, these intermediaries have associated costs that we all end up paying. Maintaining networks, employees, security systems, and payments when fraudulent operations have been carried out. To give you an idea, Visa, the company that manages card payments, had revenues in 2019 of 12 billion US dollars.

In February 2009 'Satoshi Nakamoto' wrote the following in a forum:

"The root problem with conventional currency is all the trust that's required to make it work. The central bank must be trusted not to debase the currency, but the history of fiat currencies is full of breaches of that trust. Banks must be trusted to hold our money and transfer it electronically, but they lend it out in waves of credit bubbles with barely a fraction in reserve".

Bitcoin was created at that time of distrust towards financial institutions, to create a system in which this intermediary was not needed. An innovative system in which buyers and sellers do not need to trust each other and neither an intermediary entity. A system in which buyers and sellers can trust the economic transaction by merely using this system. Not only that, but there is no central authority that can create more bitcoins at any given time due to political pressures. The creation of new bitcoins is defined in the system by a set of rules that cannot be changed. Every 10 minutes or so, new bitcoins are created, and it's going to stay that way until 21 million bitcoins have been created. At that point, no more bitcoins will be created in the system. That means there can only be 21 million bitcoins. Also, Bitcoin allows you to store your bitcoins yourself without having to go to a bank and you still are able to make digital transfers. In other words, Bitcoin is a digital currency that doesn't require a bank, it's digital cash. Bitcoin eliminates the need for banks and also central banks that are attached to governments. Bitcoin has no borders.

Bitcoin was the first cryptocurrency in history, and it introduced the technology that allows you to make these digital transfers without an intermediary entity that you have to trust. This technology is called Blockchain. You have probably heard this word before. I am not going to go into detail to describe how this technology works, as there is plenty of material for you to understand. If you are interested, I recommend you to start informing yourself on Youtube as it is easier to understand how the Blockchain works when you see it graphically. It is not a simple system, it is a distributed system, in which a network of computers around the world verify every transaction made, agree, and store the data of all transactions so that they cannot be modified, ever. Nobody can change these verified transactions because they would have to change them in all these computers (millions of them at the time of writing this book) at the same time. When a transaction is performed, a small fee has to be paid for the maintenance of these computers.

Shortly after the Bitcoin code was released and started working, other Blockchain-based cryptocurrencies began to appear. The new cryptocurrencies used different ways to validate transactions within their networks, they used different coin creation rules, with creation limits different from 21 million. Still, they were based on the same Blockchain concept. Right now, in 2020, there are thousands and thousands of cryptocurrencies. Some of them are serious projects, but many of them are projects without a strong base that will probably disappear over time. The quintessential site to explore the world of cryptocurrencies is right now, and has been for quite a few years, coinmarketcap.com. A very similar site is coingecko.com. You can use either of these two, and I'm sure there are and will be others very similar. The most important thing is that they should be independent, and their information should be entirely based on market information. In this book, we are going to talk about Coinmarketcap, but it is possible that when you read this book, Coinmarketcap has been acquired by some entity that compromises its independence. In that case, please look for a similar independent page, which does not favor any particular project. These websites offer vasts amounts of information on many different cryptocurrencies. Technical information, economic information, provides very useful graphics, information about the different markets where you can exchange a particular cryptocurrency, and it also offers historical information. We will use this page or pages quite a lot in the next chapters. This will be the first tool in your toolbox, and it's a real Swiss army knife of cryptocurrencies.

Cryptocurrencies have been born in the digital world and have been designed so that there is no need for a bank or other entity to hold this digital money. Instead, you use 'wallets' to store cryptocurrencies. In reality, cryptocurrencies are not stored anywhere. They are just information shared in the same computer network that is used to carry out and validate transactions. The network stores information about how many coins there are in each address at any moment. An address is the equivalent of a bank account. You can have several addresses on the Bitcoin network, for example, and in each address, you can store a certain number of Bitcoins. In order to move Bitcoins from one address to another (make a payment) we'll need a key, a password. The problem is that these addresses and passwords aren't easy to remember, and you can have lots of addresses for multiple cryptocurrencies, so different tools have been created to make it easier to save these addresses and passwords. These tools are called 'wallets' and exist both software wallets and hardware wallets. Software wallets are applications that are installed on your mobile phone or computer. They are convenient, and many of them are free, but if your mobile phone or computer connects to the Internet, you should be aware that there is a chance, even minimal, that they will be hacked. This has happened in the past. Hardware wallets are the most secure devices because these devices are not connected to the Internet. At the time of writing, there are two companies worldwide competing for the leadership in the hardware wallet sector: Ledger and Trezos. These two companies offer secure and easy to use devices where you can store an infinite number of cryptocurrencies.

You have to understand that many of the projects behind a cryptocurrency can be quite short-lived. There can be cryptocurrencies that simply copy others without adding any value, or there can even be projects that really have nothing behind them and are simply a scam to take money from unwary people. This market is not regulated, and therefore you can find this kind of projects. I'm not trying to scare you, but this is the reality right now. If you are going to invest in a particular cryptocurrency, it must be a serious project that has a future projection. In the next chapter, I'm going to explain how you can easily evaluate these projects using only two tools, Coinmarketcap and your common sense. And this will also be the first step to create your trading strategy: the definition of your cryptocurrency portfolio.

Chapter 4

Analyzing Cryptocurrencies

If you haven't checked out the coinmarketcap.com website yet, do it now, please. You'll see that there are thousands and thousands of cryptocurrencies. Before I continue, I would like to clarify that I have no benefit in you using this website. I simply believe that it is a must-see website right now and that, not just me, but many other investors and traders use it to get information on cryptocurrencies.

You have to understand that in 2020 the world of cryptocurrencies is very young. It is based on a technology that is still in constant evolution. Every month new projects appear, and others disappear. Therefore it is imperative to decide well in which cryptocurrencies to invest so as not to waste your money and your time. Coinmarketcap has a tool that will allow you to see with your own eyes how fast the cryptocurrency market landscape is evolving. In the tools section, you can find a link to 'Historical Snapshots'. Here you can see a history of what the ranking of cryptocurrencies was in any week since 2013 till the present. Browse through the months and years, and you will see how cryptocurrencies appear and disappear and how their prices change, and you will realize the importance of choosing wisely which cryptocurrencies to invest in.

You are probably wondering how you can know if a cryptocurrency and the project behind it are serious. You may think that you do not have sufficient knowledge about computers or economics to evaluate this type of project, but you are wrong. The tool you will need the most is your common sense. To invest, you don't need to understand perfectly how the technology behind a particular cryptocurrency works. You may not have the technical knowledge required to understand it, but even if you do, to know how each of these currencies works would require an incredible amount of time. Remember that this book is aimed at people that cannot spend the whole day reading documents and charts about cryptocurrencies, so we try to use only a small part of our time to invest in cryptocurrencies. To invest, you only need to understand what a cryptocurrency offers. It's like investing in a company. You need to understand what they are trying to solve and how. If they intend to solve a real problem that deserves to be solved and they solve it better than others, then you are in front of a project in which you can invest since it is probably a project that will not disappear very easily. From Coinmarketcap, you can access the different cryptocurrencies websites. From the website, you can get a lot of information. Use your common sense to rule out projects of dubious value. You will need to activate your critical thinking here. A faulty website with little information or a meaningless or non-existent work plan means that it is not a reliable project. You will find many like this; discard them immediately. A cryptocurrency that has survived several years (remember the Coinmarketcap history tool) may mean that the project makes sense. As a general rule, if the cryptocurrency is in the first 100 places of the Coinmarketcap ranking, it means that it has a more or less solid project and a team behind it that supports it. So... should we invest, for example, in the first 100 projects of the Coinmarketcap ranking? No. My recommendation is that you don't focus on a very extensive portfolio of cryptocurrencies, especially if you are starting in this world because it is important to know the projects in which you invest. You will need to monitor these cryptocurrencies periodically, therefore, you should select a small number of cryptocurrencies to invest in. Having a short list of cryptocurrencies to focus on will allow you to review and track them periodically to be able to make buying and selling decisions faster. Each cryptocurrency has its rules, its economy, and its development times for new features, so it's important to understand these things. For that reason, it is better to start by focusing on just a few projects, understanding them well. After that, you may want to gradually increase your knowledge by adding more cryptocurrencies to your watch list.

You should start evaluating projects right now. You will discover cryptocurrencies that you find exciting and in which you think it makes sense to invest. Create a list of those cryptocurrencies; write down on your notes why you believe each of those cryptocurrencies has a future, what solution they offer, or what is the value they are adding. This will be a living list, so I recommend that you use a spreadsheet program such as Excel or Google Sheets to make it easier for you to maintain and update the information. You can also use a word processing program if you prefer, such as Word or Google Docs.

Let's take the example of Bitcoin: Bitcoin was the first cryptocurrency created. Bitcoin introduced this new technology called Blockchain, and it's been in the market much longer than the other coins. It has had several evolutions and it is the currency used to buy other cryptocurrencies in many markets. Bitcoin itself is a revolution in the economic transactions industry. For these reasons, it should be on your list. Another example is Ethereum: Ethereum was born years after Bitcoin, but Ethereum wasn't born to be a payment method only. Ethereum is a platform. This means that Ethereum is designed so that you can create applications on the Ethereum network. These applications are called smart contracts. I am not going to explain in detail here what a smart contract is, but I do recommend that you try to do your own research and see the potential and usefulness they have. It's a utility above Bitcoin, and therefore Ethereum should also be on your list. Another example is Zcash, which was designed as a payment method very similar to Bitcoin, but Zcash provides more privacy for its users. There are other similar projects out there that offer more privacy than Bitcoin, and you should evaluate them and see which one provides a better solution to include it in your list. Dash is another cryptocurrency that improves certain aspects of Bitcoin, such as faster and cheaper transactions, with the addition that it's being used daily by many businesses around the world. As you can see, I'm giving you some examples of how to do the first analysis of a cryptocurrency and the project behind it, but it's a task you should do to familiarize yourself with the projects you're potentially going to invest your money in.

You should never have more than 20 projects on your list. Starting with a smaller list would be even better. I recommend that you start with 10 projects at most, or even less, and over time you can add more projects to your list little by little but never let this list get too long. Remember that if you have a lot of cryptocurrencies on your list, you will need too much time to periodically review and analyze each of these projects. From time to time, you will be able to explore other projects and add them to your list, and you will also most likely have to remove cryptocurrencies from your list. This list is the basis of your trading strategy.

You should also understand that the cryptocurrencies that are more established, with more time in the market and more people investing in them, tend to have less risk than newer projects or projects with fewer investors as they tend to be less volatile. This means that their price fluctuates less over time. But remember that if there is one thing that characterizes the cryptocurrency market and differentiates it from other markets, is that the volatility in general in this market is incredibly high, even for the most established projects. Still, it is interesting that you start thinking about diversifying your portfolio. I recommend that initially, and to reduce the risk, you invest a small percentage of the total in higher-risk cryptocurrencies. You should allocate a greater part of the total investment in lower-risk or more established cryptocurrencies or tokens. Over time it will be easy to understand which projects have more risk and which projects have less risk, but for now, a simple way to classify projects by risk is simply to use the Coinmarketcap ranking (remember that you can also use Coingecko or similar websites instead of Coinmarketcap). At the top of the list, you will find the most established cryptocurrencies with higher market capitalization, that is with more money invested in; therefore, these currencies are the least risky. As you advance in the ranking, you will find cryptocurrencies in which it can be riskier to invest. So it is important to have in your list cryptocurrencies from the top of the ranking, for example, from the position number 1 to 10, but it is also important that you have medium-risk cryptocurrencies; let's say from position number 10 to 40. You should also have some higher-risk cryptocurrencies; let's say from position number 40 to 100. Higher-risk cryptocurrencies have more potential to grow faster, but at the same time, they can also lose value faster. For now, I do not recommend that you consider investing in any project beyond position number 100. The reason for this is that we try to create a trading strategy with controlled risk. This way, you will be able to learn and train your capacity to suppress the reptilian brain without assuming too much risk during the process.

Before you go any further, stop reading and create your list. It is a very interesting process in which you will learn a lot, and we will also use this list to develop your trading strategy in the next chapters.

Chapter 5

Exchange Markets

Exchange markets are online sites or mobile apps where you can trade one cryptocurrency for another. In some of these markets, you can also exchange fiat currency issued by a government for a cryptocurrency. The US dollar, the Euro, or the Japanese Yen are examples of fiats. In this chapter, we will try to define in which exchange markets you will trade, that is in which markets you will carry out your buying and selling operations of cryptocurrency. Right now, there are numerous cryptocurrency exchange markets, and we can basically classify them into two types: centralized and decentralized. The big difference between the two is that in centralized markets, a company keeps your cryptocurrencies in its system. In the decentralized markets, you are the one who holds your cryptocurrencies in your own wallet. Centralized exchange markets are the more traditional markets, and their technology comes from fiat currency exchange markets or stock markets. Decentralized markets are quite a new concept and one that is still developing right now, in 2020. We have seen recently an explosion of this type of exchange. In decentralized markets, there is no central point where currencies are stored, but each user keeps his or her own cryptocurrencies.

It is important to understand that in the past, there have been some unpleasant incidents with centralized cryptocurrency exchange markets. Some of the markets have been hacked, and many people have lost all or part of the cryptocurrencies they had in these markets. Others have been very poorly managed, with corrupt owners stealing from the people who have trusted them. The truth is that the world of cryptocurrencies is a very unregulated world, where the companies behind these exchange markets do not always follow the best practices or the most ethical behaviors. One reference is MTGox. MTGox was one of the first cryptocurrency exchange markets. It was created in 2010, and in 2013-2014 it was the largest cryptocurrency exchange market in the world. In February 2014, it closed its website without notice, and shortly after that filed for bankruptcy. 850,000 Bitcoins had disappeared, at that time valued at 450 million US dollars, and the company didn't give much explanation. You can find out for yourself by merely searching the Internet for MTGox. To this day, most users have not recovered their coins. This is just one example, and I can assure you that there have been many more. Decentralized markets are more difficult to hack, but it's not impossible either. In any case, keeping your coins in an exchange market has a risk. The safest thing to do today is to keep them in your own personal wallet, hardware wallets being the safest.

HOW TO CHOOSE AN EXCHANGE MARKET

When choosing a cryptocurrency exchange market, you should consider several things:

First, if you are going to buy directly from fiat to cryptocurrency, the market you choose must accept your fiat currency. That is to say, it must have a bank account where you can send your fiat (dollars, euros..) so that once it is loaded in the system, you can buy Bitcoin, Ethereum, or the cryptocurrency of your choice. The exchange market also has to allow you to send to your fiat currency back to your bank account in case of profits or in case you simply need the money. Another thing to consider is that most of the exchange markets require you to send some personal identification information, in a process called KYC (Know Your Customer). Depending on where the exchange is located, you will have to abide by some regulations or others. Some markets may only allow users who reside in certain regions. Therefore you should choose an exchange that allows you to create an account depending on your residence.

Second, it must be a market you can trust to a certain degree. I already explained a moment ago that there is no such thing as a 100% secure exchange market. Still, there are markets that maintain their security better than others, so it is better to use markets that have a certain reputation for being secure, and that have not had major incidents or participated in scams in the past or at least in the recent past. They must offer you the best security tools to protect your account, for example, 2FA (Two Factor Authentication) is a must. Make sure also that the market keeps a significant portion of the cryptocurrencies in cold storage. Keeping coins in cold storage means that they keep a portion of their customers' coins in hardware wallets that are not connected to the Internet. This is the most secure form of storage for cryptocurrencies.

Third, you should look for cryptocurrency exchanges that have enough liquidity, especially in the cryptocurrencies you want to trade — those that you have identified in the previous chapter. This is important because it will allow you to buy or sell at the moment you want to do so. Imagine that you want to sell your Bitcoin right now, but there's no one to buy it; it could be a disaster. You can see the volume of each market for each cryptocurrency at coinmarketcap.com or coingecko.com, by clicking on the cryptocurrency name and going to the 'Market' or 'Exchange' section. These pages will allow you to see a list of existing markets, with summaries and links to their websites, and to sort the markets by volume for each of the cryptocurrencies you have chosen. These websites will be, therefore, the starting point of your research.

Fourth, you must compare the rates. Typically, centralized exchange markets do not work for free. They usually charge a small fee per trade, whether buying or selling. Many also charge a small fee when moving currencies out of their accounts. Rates vary widely among exchange markets. You can see the rates and fees on Coinmarketcap and Coingecko or similar websites. These rates are significant for day traders who do a lot of trading a year. But the strategy we're creating here won't require you to make so many trades a year, so the rates aren't that important to you, as long as they're not exaggerated. Compare the rates to see what the major markets are charging.

Fifth, ease of use. Every market has its own graphical inter-face, and they even offer price charting and technical analysis tools for trading. Some are more intuitive than others. Some you will feel more comfortable with than others, but the basic operations are the same. Also, to do technical analysis of price charts, we will use tools independent of the exchange you have chosen, so this is not a very important point.

Also, note that you can open accounts and trade in several

markets at the same time. Nothing prevents you from trading in several markets as long as you keep track of your overall account status. That is, your entire investment portfolio, regardless of whether you trade in one or three markets. My recommendation is that for the time being, you choose a maximum of three markets that meet your needs by following the above points in order. At the time of writing this book, an example of three markets with sufficient volume and variety of cryptocurrencies could be Binance, Bitfinex, and Kraken. But don't take this list from me. You must investigate on your own, as the markets can be attacked or go bankrupt at any time, so you should make your own list. This will also help you learn how to search for the necessary information and will be useful in the future, as new exchange markets will always be emerging and others disappearing. When you have your list of three markets, create an account in each one of them and set up the maximum security possible in the accounts. Remember that 2FA is a must. This will make the system verify a second time that it is you who is making the operation, either by sending a code to your email or your phone or by using some application before accessing the market or making certain operations, such as withdrawing money from your account. This makes it much more difficult to hack your account. Nowadays, many markets use a very convenient google application called Google Authenticator to enable 2FA. Security is the most important thing when creating your account in a cryptocurrency exchange market. It is also important that you understand that due to regulations, account creation could take some time because they will need to verify certain data, especially if you want to send or receive 'fiat' from an exchange market. This can take several days, depending on the market. Therefore I think it is good to have several accounts open so that if necessary, you can immediately move currencies to another market. Even if you have chosen three markets, and have accounts open in all three, my recommendation is that you start trading and become familiar with only one if possible. As you gain more experience, you can easily move from one market to another to take advantage of different situations.

III

Building Your Trading Strategy

In the second part of the book, you have built the foundation of your strategy. In this third part we will explore various aspects of your trading strategy such as portfolio management, when to buy, when to sell, indicators that can help you in these decisions, position size, risk control strategies, and, above all, how to control your reptilian brain so that it does not prevent you from following your strategy.

Chapter 6

Reptile Emotions

This is probably the most important chapter in the book. I know you want to start understanding how to analyze charts and which tools to use, but listen to me: read this chapter. You may already know or suspect what I'm going to tell you. But I insist. Read it. Twice. Five times. As many times as it takes to not only understand it but interiorize it.

Learning to read the daily charts, understanding the different indicators, learning to control the risk of the trades is going to be the easiest thing in learning to trade. The most complicated thing, by far, will be controlling your emotions, controlling your reptilian fear and greed at key moments. You can have the best strategy in the world, you can know all the indicators, all the oscillators and all the figures and identify them correctly on the charts, but if when the time comes, your reptilian brain takes control, I can assure you that you will not follow your own strategy and you will make decisions that are not based on lógic, with disastrous long-term consequences.

The trading strategy that we are going to design together is a strategy designed to reduce stress in these key moments.

Designing a complicated strategy makes no sense if you can't follow it, so we will always try to keep it simple. Your trading strategy will be based exclusively on technical analysis to elim-inate the influence of emotions as much as possible. We will analyze charts using different, very simple free tools available to anyone, and we will make decisions based ONLY on this analysis. Today, we are continually bombarded with information. With news from all over the world on Youtube or on investment forums and chats. You must stay away from all that. All that information is only going to affect your emotions, making your reptilian brain stronger and your neocortex weaker. It's your money. You must decide for yourself using a strategy adapted to your situation and your personality.

Get this into your head: No one can guess the future. No one. Traders who make money don't guess prices. They simply have a strategy that plays with the odds in their favor, and in this way, they make money in the long run. But all traders make trades in which they lose money. It's inevitable. Let's say you follow the best trader in the world on Youtube or Twitter. He will tell you his opinions and ideas, based on his knowledge and experience, his personality and his way of trading. These ideas will most likely not work for you. But the reality is much worse. The Internet is full of individuals and companies publishing their ideas on any platform. The vast majority of them do it with the idea of making a profit from these publications. That is, the more people read the article or news, the more people watch the video, the more money they make. Therefore, the vast majority of this content is directed to make you click, and the easiest for them to make you click is through your emotions. That's why all these articles and videos always try to pick you fear or greed. In addition to that, many of these companies and individuals are dedicated to selling classes, courses, or trading signals. What I mean is that the primary goal of these news, videos, and articles is not that you learn or that you make money, but that you click so that they can make money.

Many people want to become a trader to get rich. The truth is that most of them end up losing money. And of the few traders who do make money, very few get rich. Most traders who make money don't have millions and millions in the bank. They may live more or less comfortably, they may have their independence, etc. but they are not millionaires. Of course there are exceptions, but if that's your idea, get it out of your head right now. In this book we will create a strategy to minimize your emotions at a time when you are starting to invest. For instance, an essential part of this strategy to minimize your emotions of fear and greed will be to make small trades. I can assure you right now that your reptilian brain (greed) is going to push you to make bigger trades. At that moment you will notice the force that your reptilian brain has on your neocortex. Resist! Don't fall. If you do operations that are too big, your reptilian brain will continue to dominate throughout the whole trade, making you sell too soon or too late, and most importantly, you will have lost an opportunity to learn and improve your control over the reptilian brain. As time goes by, you will be able to make bigger trades, but for the moment, it is critical to start with small operations.

In the next chapters, we will talk about technical analysis, like price chart analysis, and as you learn how to trade and how to use new tools, you will build a trading strategy adapted to yourself.

Chapter 7

Charts

We have already seen that in order to avoid falling into the reptilian brain's clutches and doing operations based on our emotions, we are going to base our strategy entirely on technical analysis. We will not pay attention and give too much importance to the constant flow of news in the world of economics and cryptocurrencies. That would only increase the strength of your reptilian brain and your emotions, and therefore it would be very risky.

Technical analysis allows us, through a series of tools, to consolidate an enormous amount of information on prices and past operations in order to make decisions. I want to be very clear about one thing. Technical analysis is not a crystal ball, it does not make you see the future. Technical analysis is based on seeing how the market has behaved in the past in a situation similar to the present. It is more likely that if the market has behaved many times in one way in the past, it will behave similarly again in the future. But we always talk about probabilities. Let me give you a simple example so that you understand how it works and why we use it. Suppose we find ourselves in a particular market situation, for example, the price of Bitcoin has dropped 10% quickly and has remained stable for a few days. Now you want to know what will happen in the next few days or weeks. You want to know if the price of Bitcoin is going to go up again or keep going down after this fall. Having many years of price and trading history of a particular market at our fingertips, we can look for similar situations in the past. We will probably find several similar situations over the years, let's say we find 100 similar situations in the price history. Analyzing these 100 similar situations we see that in 76 of them, the price, after a few days went back up to similar levels from where it was before it fell. On the other 24 occasions, the Bitcoin price continued to fall. So we see that when we have been in a similar situation in the past, in most cases the price has gone up again. Does this mean that the price will go up? No. We can't predict the future. Even if we look at the charts and see that out of 100 times something similar happened the price went up again every time, that does not mean that it will go up this time. We can never be sure. Technical analysis is not an exact science. It can guide us to make decisions based on the past, but we always have to take into account that there is a risk factor and we have to put structures in our strategy to control that risk. It is simply a game of probabilities.

The goal of our strategy is to make money. We don't need to predict exactly what is going to happen with the price to make money. A strategy has to be based on risk and probability, not on beliefs.

CHARTING SOFTWARE

To visualize the price charts we need specialized software. I assume you have a computer. Although you can trade with your mobile phone, chart analysis requires a large enough screen. It doesn't have to be anything very powerful as all the tools we are going to use are web-based, so you will only need a web browser.

In 2020, the leader in online price charting software is TradingView. You can access this software through its website tradingview.com. With access to the biggest markets, not only cryptocurrencies, but also stocks, futures, indices, forex... it is a very complete software with all the indicators you will need. On top of that, you don't have to install anything, it's completely online. The free version will allow you to perform a fairly extensive analysis. They offer a paid version that allows you to add more indicators and is even more complete. For example, with the paid version you can put multiple alerts, which is quite useful. TradingView can be integrated with some exchange markets to trade cryptocurrencies but there are very few options. But don't worry, this is not a problem. For the kind of strategy we are designing here, where we are not going to make many trades per month and we do not really care about the short-term fluctuations of price -minutes-, you can do the analysis in TradingView and at the moment of making the trades, make them directly on the exchange market website. There are other chart analysis pages. If you are looking for something completely free, Gocharting.com is an alternative to TradingView. It is a new project and it's under development, so it doesn't have the same functionalities as TradingView at the moment.

There is specialized software that can connect to your accounts in the exchange markets to centralize the operations. This can be useful when trading in multiple markets simultaneously. They are also useful because they help you maintain a global history of your trades. One of the most widely used today is Coinigy, but there are several similar ones. All the software that connects to your trading market accounts is usually paid for. I don't know of any free ones that you can trust. Think about allowing this software to access your trading accounts for trading. In my opinion, and for the type of strategy we are designing, you are not going to need to rely on software like Coinigy, although, of course, it can have its advantages and it is something you can consider in making an investment in the future.

You should keep a trading history or trading log. Even if you make few trades, think that it can take weeks or even months from a buy operation to a sell operation so you can't rely on your memory. You will need this history, along with your notes, to analyze the status of your open trades on a regular basis. Also, this will help you to build your self-discipline. As I said before, there is software that makes an automatic history, connecting to your accounts. You can also keep this history in TradingView or Gocharting and similar applications, usually under the option 'Paper Trading'. My recommendation is that you use a simple spreadsheet to get started, for example, Microsoft Excel or Google Sheets, where you can put your notes, add images and screenshots with your chart analysis and update them as the trade progresses. This will require a little more work on your part, but it will also make you include an element of discipline when performing your operations, and as you will see in the last part of the book, you will need this history to evolve your strategy.

I assume you've seen price charts before. For the rest of this chapter, we'll talk about the basics. If you already have experience with price charts, you can go straight to the next chapter where we'll start talking about analysis.

Price charts allow us to see how prices evolve over time. In cryptocurrency analysis, we will be analyzing currency pairs in a specific exchange market. Currencies, just like stocks, have an abbreviated code in the exchange market. For instance, Bitcoin is usually BTC, Ethereum is usually ETH, Euro is usually EUR, and US Dollar is USD. If we want to see the Bitcoin price in US dollars, we'll look for the Bitcoin/USD price chart. If we write 'BTCUSD' in the search engine of our price chart analysis software, we will get a list of possible charts, as there are several exchange markets that allow you to trade this pair of currencies. The software will allow you to search by market. If you search in Tradingview or Gocharting or similar, you will get a list similar to this one:

Code | Description | Market

BTCUSD | Bitcoin / US Dollar | Bitstamp

BTCUSD | BTC/USD | Coinbase

...

If we trade the BTCUSD pair, we will be exchanging US Dollars for Bitcoin or the other way around. But in these markets we can also exchange one cryptocurrency for another cryptocurrency. For example, imagine we have a certain amount of Bitcoin. Suppose we now want to use our Bitcoin to buy Ethereum. We want to buy

Ethereum with Bitcoin, so to see the price chart of this pair we will look for ETHBTC and a list will appear similar to the previous one, but with the markets that offer this particular pair.

Now, let's practice a bit: open a price chart, no matter what pair, and we will explain the basic tools. First, you will see that the chart has a periodicity, top left, you can see D (Day), W (Week), M (Month), and then a few hour options, like 4h, 2h, 1h, and so on up to 1 minute. The periodicity indicates how often the chart is painted. Larger periodicities such as D, W, and M allow you to see more history information on the screen. Smaller ones such as hours and minutes allow you to see the detail of a much shorter period of time. Depending on your strategy and your type of trading you will use some periodicities more than others. For example, a day trader will use much more minute periodicities, and a longer-term trader will use Day, Week, and Month periodicities without ever paying attention to the hours or minutes.

Right next to the periodicity you will see the type of lines on the chart. Most likely the default option is 'Candles'. They are called candles because they look like some sort of candles if you take a good look. These are the most used ones and the ones that I recommend to start with for the type of strategy that we are going to design here in this book, therefore I am not going to explain the operation of all the others, like the bars, areas, kagi... If later on you want to go into other ways of trading like day trading you might be interested in investigating other types of candles like Heikin Ashi candles. In the following image, you can see a description of what each part of the candle means. The candles will depend on the periodicity chosen. For the next example, we will assume that we have chosen a periodicity of 1 day. The color of the candle will be green if the closing price of the day is higher than the opening price, that is, if the price has risen during the day. The candle will be red if the price has fallen, i.e. if the opening price is higher than the closing price. The difference between the opening and closing price will define the body of the candle. But the price can vary during the day, sometimes, quite a bit above and/or below the opening and closing price. This price change forms the upper and lower wicks.

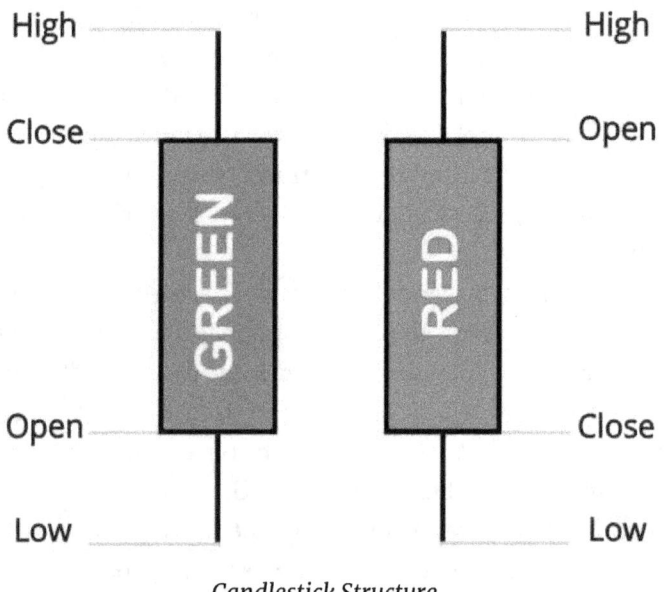

Candlestick Structure

This structure offers us a significant amount of information in a very concentrated way, that is why it has been traditionally used in price charts. For our initial analysis, we can also use line charts. Line charts provide less information than candlestick charts but are sufficient for an initial analysis as we will see in the next chapter. Line charts simply mark the price at a given time, usually the closing price. Depending on the period chosen this could be the price at the moment of closing the day, the hour, the minute... In the chart below we can see a line chart of the BTCUSD pair. The periodicity is daily, so the line we see is constructed by the Bitcoin price in US dollars at the close of each day from the year 2013 to the present.

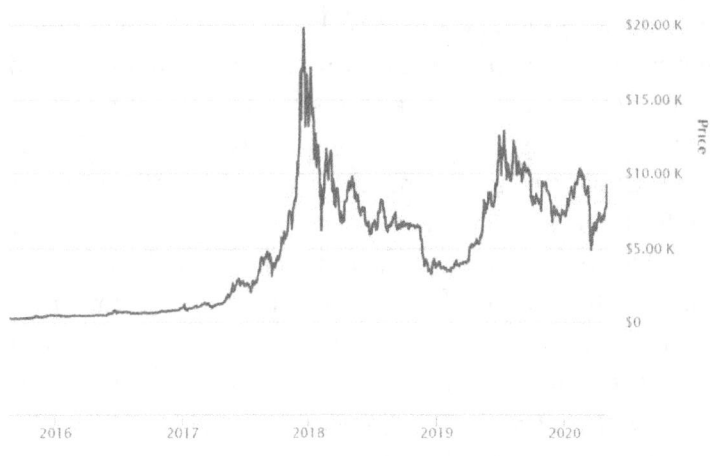

Bitcoin price line chart in US dollars extracted from Coinmarketcap

Now you have to choose which pairs you want to invest in. You can use Coinmarketcap or Coingecko to see a list of the different pairs and on which exchange markets they are offered. Depending on the cryptocurrency, you will have a pair with some fiat currency – or with some cryptocurrency with a value pegged to fiat, like USDT, EURT, USDCoin, Binance USD... there are many

- or there may only be pairs with Bitcoin or with Ethereum. In the latter case, it means that you will need to buy Bitcoin or Ethereum first to access this market. Because your project list has been designed to have a majority of established projects, you should find pairs with fiat currencies from the vast majority of projects on your list. To begin with, it's easier to trade fiat pairs because if you trade BTC or Ethereum pairs you should be watching the movements of these cryptocurrencies as they can have moments of high price variability.

Regardless of the periodicity selected, the charts allow us to zoom in to focus on a certain period of time. If you haven't already done so, play a little with the price charts at different periodicities for the cryptocurrencies you have selected in chapter 4. Use the charting software you have chosen, such as TradingView, but you should also learn how to use the Coinmarketcap or Coingecko charts and similar pages to perform the initial analysis. At this point you don't need to understand everything, just play around with the options and different tools offered by the different services to familiarize yourself before diving on the technical analysis in the next chapters. Start with the 1-day periodicity and see where the price is right now. See if the price has been going down or up in the last month. Move to a weekly frequency and try to locate the highest price ever. Write it down on your list. Now try to locate the minimum price. Look for currency pairs related to the fiat currency you are going to use, for example BTCUSD or BTCEUR. Now look for related cryptocurrency pairs from the list you made in chapter 4, for example, XMRBTC or ETHBTC. Look at the candles, the bodies, and the wicks. See how far the wicks have gone, and the difference between the body. This will help you start to get a good handle on price charts and easily navigate from one pair to another. In the next few chapters, we will start doing some technical analysis, so you need to be able to move easily between price pairs and understand the periodicities and structure of the candles before you proceed.

Chapter 8

Resistance - Support and Trends

If you had to choose only one tool for trading, this would be the one you would choose without any doubt. The more you perfect your ability to find resistance and support in the price charts, the more likely you are to make successful trades. In the strategy we are designing we will use this knowledge combined with indicators to decide entry and exit points for trades, therefore we have to address it in this first chapter that we are talking about technical analysis, and it is very important that you practice to be able to find resistance and support levels in a chart with just a glance. You should be able to find these levels using line charts or candlestick charts. I'm going to give you some basic rules for finding these levels, but first, let's define them.

As you have seen from the price charts, the price never goes up or down in a straight line, but it rather moves in waves. It goes up for a while until it reaches a price, and then it starts to go down until it finds another price, and then it goes up again and so on. This is due to the forces of buying and selling at every moment, that is, the law of supply and demand. If at a given moment there are many people who want to buy Bitcoin and very few want to sell it, the price of Bitcoin will go up. If for any reason there are many people who want to sell their Bitcoin and there are few people who want to buy it, then the price will go down. This is the basis for all price action; the only reason why prices go up or down.

A resistance is a level in the price where we see that it resists going up and even when it reaches that price, it turns around and starts going down. Continuing with the wave analogy, the resistance would be the crest of the wave. A support is the opposite of a resistance. A price level where the price, when it is falling, stops its fall and even goes back up again. It would be the lowest point of the wave. These levels are not exact price levels. They act more like a spring and form zones. If the price is rising, we see that as we approach a resistance level there is more and more selling force; as we squeeze a spring, it becomes more and more forceful in the opposite direction, until there comes a point where the price stops rising and falls. The same thing happens with the supports, so we can imagine the resistance and supports as invisible springs that affect the price as it goes up and down.

Resistances and supports can be broken. If the price action is strong enough, it can break a resistance easily. Remember, this is not an exact science. We are always talking about probabilities. Therefore when we identify a support or resistance it does not mean that we are 100% sure that the support or resistance will stop the price action, but rather that there is a higher probability that the price action will change at those levels.

So how can we identify these levels? The only information we have to identify levels of resistance and support is price history. So to find them we have to look at the price charts and find areas where the price has encountered these invisible springs in the past. We can find support and resistance by looking at any periodicity. To look for resistance levels in the past, let's look for situations where the price was rising and found a spring, a top. Maybe the price stayed at that level for a while or went down again, but it didn't go through. We can identify resistance levels because we see that the price reaches the resistance level and can't go above it several times, some times further apart in time than others. Sometimes it goes over the resistance level but comes back quickly, imitating that spring action. To identify supports we will look for exactly the same price action but in the opposite direction, i.e. when prices are falling. The support or resistance will be stronger the more times we can see that it has managed to stop the price movement. We can also measure the strength of a support or resistance using time. For example, if we see that the BTCUSD price has been trying to pass $6,500 for three months in the past, but has been trying to pass $1,000 for eight months, then we can assume that the $1,000 resistance is stronger than the $6,500 resistance.

Easy, right? But there's more. Supports and resistances have a very important feature. When price action breaks through a resistance, this resistance level immediately becomes a support and vice versa. In the example above, if the BTCUSD has been trying to break the $1,000 resistance for eight months, once the price action breaks the resistance, it will turn into a support. And we can see this happening over and over again on the charts. Many times when a strong resistance is broken, we see how the price, after a rise, goes back down to the same levels of resistance, in this case already converted into support, and then continues to rise. In the image below we can see the ETHUSD price chart extracted from Coinmarketcap, where we can see more than four years of price information. Please go to

Coinmarketcap or Coingecko or some similar page, open this chart and try to find the highest levels of support and resistance.

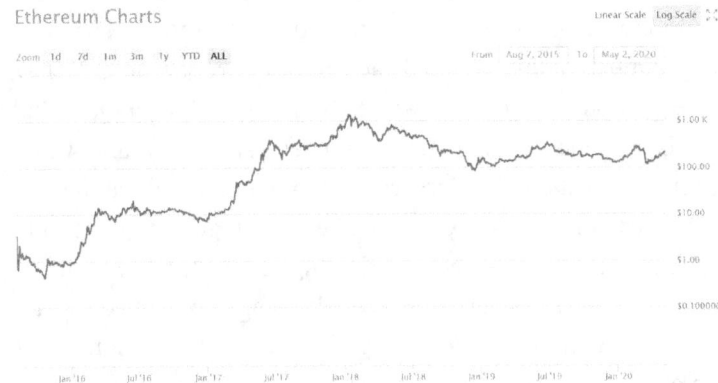

ETHUSD price chart on coinmarketcap

With just a quick analysis, we see that Ethereum, after a few months at the $1 resistance, quickly moved to the $10 level. The $10 level remained important as support for a year. Once that support was consolidated, Ethereum moved up and seemed to have briefly found resistance around the $50 level. The $100 level was a very brief resistance around May–June 2017, but we see that in early 2019 Ethereum revisited the $100 level, which this time had become support. This quick analysis that we have done is at a very high level. We can do a similar analysis by looking at a shorter period of time, this way we will be more accurate in finding support and resistance levels, but remember that support and resistance levels are not an exact price, but rather price zones.

To get some more practice, you can do the same exercise as above but with pairs from the list of cryptocurrencies you created in chapter 4, and if you want, with some more. You have already found highs and lows, now it's time to find support and resistance levels. Surely by now you have noticed that many times the support and resistance levels coincide with round numbers, such as 10, 100, 200, 1000, 2000... especially in the most popular pairs of each cryptocurrency like BTCUSD, ETHUSD, etc. This is simply due to human psychology. Our mind tends to round off numbers for simplicity and many times when putting buy and sell orders we tend to select round numbers.

If you think about it, you can take advantage of supports and resistances to make trades with a higher probability of profit. For example, imagine that you are looking at one of your pairs selected in Chapter 4. You see that the price takes a significant amount of time trying to break a certain resistance. You see that the price has been trying to break a resistance for a long time. Finally it breaks it, goes up a little and then falls back to the resistance levels identified earlier. But you know that now that resistance level has become a support. You can deduce that if that support is confirmed — it holds the pressure of the price decline — in the future the price will rise again because now there is no resistance. This is just a very simple example. You can also identify future resistances to identify possible points to take profit from a trade.

Another key concept is the trend. As we have seen before, prices never go up in a straight line, but rather form waves. They go up, form the crest of the wave and go back down a bit, then go back up and mark a higher price than the previous crest, then go back down. When the peaks of the waves are higher and higher, and especially the lower parts of the waves are also higher, this means that we are in an upward trend. An upward trend will generate higher prices every time. On the other hand, if the low parts of the waves are getting lower, and especially the crests of the waves are getting lower, this means that we are in a downward trend, therefore we will see lower and lower prices.

BTCUSD in a downward trend – line chart

In the image of the BTCUSD chart extracted from Coinmarketcap, we can see several months of prices in a line chart. We see how the wave crests, which I marked with horizontal lines, are getting lower and lower. Clearly, the market for BTCUSD is in a downward trend. But we can see something strange. I have chosen this chart because in it we can see the difference between line charts and candlestick charts very clearly, and we can see how the candlestick charts contain more information. On the line chart above we can see how in mid–February 2020 there is a higher crest than the previous one. But when we analyze the same price chart but this time using a daily candlestick chart, in this case, extracted from TradingView (please open the BTCUSD chart in TradingView and make sure you are seeing a daily candlestick chart. Zoom in until you see the period between

June 2019 and April 2020) we see that between February and March 2020 the price reached exactly the same point as at the end of October 2019. What happens is that at the end of October 2019 the price went up to $10,500 and went down again within the same day. We can see this in the candlestick chart because the candlestick tells us both the high of the day and the low, but this information is lost in a line chart, because the price marked on the line does not have to be the high of the day, but is usually the closing price of the day which is the price at 00:00 UTC. This is why I recommend using candlestick charts for more detailed price analysis.

BTCUSD in a downward trend – candlestick chart

We can find trends in any periodicity. Trends that last minutes or a few hours, trends that last a few days, trends that last a few weeks, months, and even multiple years. The job of a trader is simply to take advantage of those trends, and the duration of the trend you choose will determine the type of trader you are. Day traders choose short-term trends, minutes or hours. Investors choose much longer trends of many months or years. In our strategy, we will choose intermediate trends, of several weeks and even a few months. Therefore we will basically work on charts with a periodicity between 1 day and a week that will allow us to see these types of trends more clearly. This way we can benefit from large price movements without being long-term investors.

We say that a downward trend has been broken, or changed, when a high (crest of the wave) is higher than the previous high. In the above BTCUSD chart, the downward trend was not broken because the mid-February 2020 wave crest reached exactly the same point as the previous high of late October 2019 but did not surpass it, and we can see how it continued to fall further after that. To break an upward trend, the situation is reversed. The price must create a lower low than the previous one.

As a task to perform, before going on to the next chapter, you should have analyzed all the charts of your chosen trading pairs in chapter 4. Use daily candlestick charts to analyze them. You already have highs and lows noted, now find the highest supports and resistances of each. See if the price is currently at or near any major support, also identify if they are in an upward or downward trend. Move to the weekly chart and go back to analyze the trends in this periodicity. The weekly chart will give you a broader perspective. Write this down in your spreadsheet or word processing file for each of the chosen pairs. In the next chapter, we will finally talk about how to start trading — how to buy and sell cryptocurrencies—, but for this, you must be clear about how to identify supports and resistances so it is important that you have done at least the exercise I have just proposed to get enough practice. If after doing the exercise you still have problems finding supports and resistances or identifying trends, you should practice more. You live in the information age. You have access to an infinite number of price charts, guides and tutorials on Youtube and other platforms, and for free. Use these tools and practice as much as you need, see you in the next chapter!

Chapter 9

Orders: Number, Size and Risk

When we talk about orders we mean buying and selling orders. At this point in the book, you should already have a list of the cryptocurrencies or pairs you have decided to trade, along with basic technical and fundamental analysis information for each, all noted in a spreadsheet, word processing file, or similar tool. We have the reasons why we find the chosen projects interesting and why we see a future for them (chapter 4), we have noted historical high and low price data (chapter 7), and we have identified important supports and resistances and market trends (chapter 8). In addition we also have a short list of exchange markets where we are going to trade (chapter 5) and you have created accounts in these markets. As you can see, we have already covered much ground. Well done! If you haven't done any of these tasks yet, stop reading right now, go back and do them. you are going to need them for this chapter and the next ones.

In this chapter we are going to take a very important step in designing our trading strategy. We are going to design our trading orders: How big they are going to be, that is how much money we are going to use to buy a cryptocurrency, how many trades we are going to make, approximately, in a period of time and how many trades we should have open at the same time. At all times we will make decisions to minimize risk and to dominate our reptilian brain. In general, you have to design a strategy that allows you to operate without your reptilian brain taking control and this varies from one person to another so you have to design it yourself as it has to be tailored for you.

The first thing you have to decide is how much money you are going to invest in cryptocurrencies in total. This will be the initial size of your portfolio. The only goal is that, over time, the size of your portfolio grows. Your goal is not to guess the price of Bitcoin next week. Your goal is to grow your portfolio. No one can tell you what your investment in cryptocurrencies should be. That will depend entirely on you, your savings, your other investments, your ability to take risks, and your belief in the future of this technology. For example, you may want to invest a portion of your savings in precious metals and another portion in cryptocurrencies. Here I can only give you one recommendation: invest only what you can afford to lose. An amount that in case of complete loss would not change your lifestyle. No matter how much we try to minimize the risk, investing always has a risk. My recommendation is that you should always have some mattress savings, which should not be touched just in case. These savings should allow you to live a while without working. From there on it is entirely up to you how much you allocate to investing in cryptocurrencies. Think about that number and write it down. Remember that it should be a sum of money that if you lose it completely does not change your lifestyle. This is your initial portfolio size.

Do you remember when the reptilian brain is activated? The

reptilian brain treats money as a basic good necessary for life. The more money you are using to buy or sell in a transaction, the more control your reptilian brain will have over your actions. Therefore, to mitigate the power of the reptilian brain, we have to operate with small amounts at first. Imagine that we identify a possible purchase operation in one of the cryptocurrencies we are monitoring. We already have our portfolio size. Are we going to use all our money on that first operation? NO. That would be too much and our reptilian brain would take over with unforeseeable consequences. Plus that would represent a huge risk. Remember that no matter how much technical analysis we do, no matter how much we trust a project, no one can guess the future. You must always be prepared to lose. Instead of using all our money, we will be trading with much smaller quantities. Take your portfolio size and divide it by 10. What number does that give you? Do you still think it's a very large sum of money? Then divide it by 15. That number you are comfortable with is going to be the size of your trade initially. As your portfolio grows, this number will grow as well, and as your experience increases and you learn to take control of your reptilian brain, you will be able to modify the size of the trade according to certain circumstances, but I recommend that you start by dividing your portfolio by a number between 10 and 15, and never less than 10. When you make your trade, you will use this amount. That means that to invest all the money you want to invest you will need to make 10 to 15 buy trades. But be careful, when you identify a good time to buy, I assure you that you will think about skipping this rule and buying more: Don't do it. This is your reptilian brain at work, your greed. Remember, no matter how convinced you are, this is not an exact science. No one can be 100% sure of price movements. What we are doing with this small order size is controlling your emotions, controlling your reptilian brain while you gain experience in doing operations. If you break this rule and make a trade that is too big, the first time the price drops a little, you will start to have doubts, and consider selling. Even more so if, when you perform the operation, the price begins to drop immediately. This can and will happen to you on more than one occasion. You need to keep your reptilian brain under control for the whole trade, so it is better to do small operations. This will also allow you to do more operations and each operation you do is an opportunity to learn and gain experience. You will have time to do bigger operations, believe me, but it is very important that you start with small operations.

Order Types

When we put an order, it can be a buy or a sell. If we're in the BTCUSD market for example, if we buy Bitcoin we would pay in US dollars and we would receive Bitcoin. For this, we should have US dollars in our account. To sell in the same pair we would sell Bitcoin and receive US dollars. So far it's clear, it's like buying bread. But the reality is that in these markets we can buy and sell in different ways than in the bakery. The exchange market works by matching sell orders with buy orders. That is, you can set the price at which you want to buy or sell. The price you see on the charts is the price of the last buy/sell operation made in the market. That's why the price is constantly changing. Let's say the BTC price is $8,962.7 right now on the exchange you have chosen. But in reality, there are many people who have placed their buy and sell order and are waiting for someone else to agree to buy or sell at the same price they have placed. You can see all the active orders on the market in the Order Book. In the image, you can see the first rows of the BTCUSD pair Order Book on the Kraken.com exchange. In the next image, we only show the Buying orders for improved readability, but in the exchange markets, you can see both the Buying and the Selling orders. The order book is the state of the market at any given time and it's constantly changing. We will use this order book to explain the basic operations we can perform.

New & Open Orders	Positions		Order Book	
		Buying		
Cm. Vol. ⬍	Cm. Cost ⬍	Cost ⬍	Volume ⬍	Price ▾
0.100	$896.3	$896.3	0.100	$8,962.5
0.600	$5,376.7	$4,480.4	0.500	$8,960.7
0.646	$5,788.9	$412.2	0.046	$8,960.5
0.870	$7,796.0	$2,007.1	0.224	$8,960.4
1.094	$9,803.1	$2,007.1	0.224	$8,960.3
5.094	$45,643.9	$35,840.8	4.000	$8,960.2

First BTCUSD buying orders from the Kraken order book

Market Orders. In this image, we see that the first buy order is at the price of $8,962.5 (in the 'Price' column). We also see that at that price they are willing to buy 0.1 BTC (the second column from the right of that same table, with the title 'Volume'). The cost of that operation, if it were done, would be $896.3 (the third column from the right, 'Cost'). The second buy order (in the second row of the table) we see that it is at a slightly lower price, $8,960.7, and they are willing to buy up to 0.5 BTC. This means that if we have BTC and we want to sell it, the highest market price right now is $8,962.5, and at that price they are only willing to buy 0.1 BTC. If we want to sell 1 BTC right now we would have to sell 0.1 BTC at $8,962.5, 0.5 BTC at $8,960.7, 0.046 BTC at $8,960.5, and so on until we sell the whole Bitcoin, reaching the fifth row of the table with the price of $8,960.3. If we wanted to sell 5 BTCs right now we would do the same exercise but in this case, we would get to the last row of the table. This is called a market sell and the software does it automatically if we indicate that we want to sell 5 BTCs to the market for example. It works exactly the same way for market buy, but in this case, we will look at the Selling order table.

Selling

Price ▲	Volume ⇕	Cost ⇕	Cm. Cost ⇕	Cm. Vol. ⇕
$8,962.7	1.100	$9,859.0	$9,859.0	1.100
$8,962.8	0.045	$403.3	$10,262.3	1.145
$8,963.2	2.281	$20,445.1	$30,707.4	3.426
$8,963.3	4.000	$35,853.2	$66,560.6	7.426
$8,964.8	0.278	$2,492.2	$69,052.8	7.704
$8,965.0	1.755	$15,733.6	$84,786.4	9.459

First BTCUSD selling orders from the Kraken order book

Let's imagine that our order size that we have previously calculated is $10,000. Remember that this would mean that our portfolio size is $100,000 or more. If we put a market order to buy $10,000 of BTC at this point, we will be buying 1.1 BTC at $8,962.7 per BTC at a cost of $9,859, and the rest, i.e. $10,000 - $9,859 = $141, will be used to buy BTC at the price of $8,962.8 (the second row of the table). This means that we would receive 1.1 BTC from the first row, and 0.01573 BTC from the second row for a total of 1.11573 BTC. We would have exchanged $10,000 for 1,11573 BTC. Don't panic, you don't have to do these calculations yourself. The exchange software takes care of everything. Buying or selling to market is the simplest operation. You simply say how much you want to buy or sell and the software takes care of the rest. I'm explaining this to you because I think it's important that you understand how exchange markets really work, and this applies to any market, not just the cryptocurrency market.

Limit Orders. Limit buy orders or limit sell orders. This type of order is used when you want to select the limit price at which you want to buy or sell. As we have just seen, when you buy or sell using a market order, you cannot choose the price at which you buy or sell. The trade price will depend on the orders in the order book at that time. Limit trading allows you to specify a price. When you create a limit order, what you are doing is writing a row in the order book. For example, if we want to buy 0.2 BTC at $8,962.6 at the most, we will make a limit trade for that price and that will create a new row in the order book. In this case, between the first and second row of the Buying order table, a new row will be added with our order. It is important to understand that when we place a limit order in the market like this, we have to wait until there is another sell order at the same price or a market sell order with enough volume, for the order to be executed, that is, for the trade to occur and we will receive in this case the 0.2 BTC we wanted to buy. I can place a buy order for 0.2 BTC at the price of $1,000, but if there is no one willing to sell their BTC at that price, it will not be executed. Sell limit orders work exactly the same way. If I want to sell my 0.2 BTC, but at least I want to sell it at $8,964, I would place a sell limit order at that price and this would generate a new row in the order book between the fourth and fifth row in the sell order table.

As we have seen, for both market and limit orders, we are interested in trading in markets where there are a lot of people buying and selling, if not, we can have some problems such as a market trade being executed at a very different price from the current one, or a limit trade not being executed at all. This is why I recommend in chapter 5 to always trade using markets and pairs with a lot of volume, also called liquidity. Remember that you can see the volume of the pairs for each market in Coinmarketcap and similar pages. Review chapter 5 if necessary.

A note about fees: As you know, the exchange markets usually make money through fees they put on certain trades. In many markets, these two order types have different fees when executed. Typically, market order fees are a little higher than limit order fees. These are called maker fees and taker fees. The difference is usually minimal, so in my opinion, this is not a reason to choose one type of order over another. Also, with the type of strategy we're designing we won't make many trades so the fees aren't that important. Anyway, as I explain in chapter 5, you should choose exchange markets with competitive fees.

Apart from market and limit orders, there are other types of orders that can be very useful, especially when combined, such as stop loss and take profit orders. A stop loss order is designed to stop the losses of a trade. Remember that this is not an exact science, we are talking about probabilities. Any trade, no matter how good your strategy is, has a chance of going wrong. Also, at any time there can be a crisis or any news that makes the price drop quickly and can put your trades at a loss. The market is open 24 hours a day. You can't be watching the price continuously and even if you could, watching the price constantly is only going to make your reptilian brain take over, and as you know, that's the last thing we want to happen. Stop loss orders allow us to set a price where if it is exceeded, a sell order will automatically be generated, usually a market order. This allows us to define an exit strategy in case the operation does not go as we had planned.

Stop loss is therefore like a safety net and helps us to reduce the risk of important losses. So every time one of your buy orders is executed, you should place a stop loss order to reduce the risk of important losses. A take profit order will also automatically sell when the price reaches a certain point that we can specify, but in this case, it is a profitable trade, that is when the price goes up. This is useful in some strategies, where you define at the moment of buying, the price at which you are going to sell in the future. Take profit makes sense in combination with stop loss to automate the exit of a trade, whether it is a profit or a loss. In the next chapters, we will define at what price you should set these orders. For now, you just need to understand what each order type is for.

Not all exchange markets allow you to put the same types of orders. Market and limit orders are the basic ones, but from there you can find markets that offer more or fewer types of trades or that allow you to combine trades or not. It is important that you read the documentation of the exchange markets you have chosen, where they explain how to trade on their systems. The way to trade and the restrictions may vary from market to market, but the basis is always the same. It is important that you learn how to trade in your chosen exchange markets in chapter 5, and that you understand what types of orders you have available in each one. When it's time to buy or sell, you don't want to be looking at the documentation, so do this in advance. If you see that one of the exchange markets you have chosen does not allow you to put stop loss orders, then you should reconsider using that exchange. Remember that a stop loss allows you to reduce the risk of major losses, and any risk reduction is good for our strategy.

Every time you make a trade you should write it down in your trade history log. A spreadsheet or a word processing file is perfect for this. You should at least write down the pair, the exchange market, the date, the price at which the purchase was made, the stop loss price you have set up to reduce the risk, and the notes of your expectations and exit strategy. Don't worry if you don't have all this clear right now, it will become much clearer in the next chapters. Keeping track of your trades will allow you to look back and analyze how your strategy is working in the future so you can learn what works for you and evolve it over time.

Portfolio management. As you can see, reducing risk is always important in a trading strategy. We have just seen how we can reduce risk in the way we set up our trading orders. But there are more ways to reduce our risk in general. We introduced the idea, in chapter 4, that more established projects have less risk, they are less volatile and a little more predictable, partly because they have more trading volume. Newer, smaller projects tend to have more price variation and very rapid price movements. Considering that this price variation is in itself very large in the whole cryptocurrency market, including the more established currencies, in my opinion, it is very risky to create a strategy based on buying only new and not very established cryptocurrencies. They are more unpredictable, more variable, and therefore increase the overall risk of the strategy. When you start making purchases, you will be accumulating cryptocurrencies, that is, you will be investing in these projects. Therefore it is important that you always keep an eye on which projects you are investing in at any given time. We are going to establish some basic rules for portfolio management with the idea of maximizing the profit without increasing the risk too much. To do this, we're going to use the list of projects you created in Chapter 4, which I hope you'll keep up to date. Your investment portfolio will be the list of cryptocurrencies you have at any given time. For each cryptocurrency, you must calculate what percentage it represents of your total portfolio. In order to do that, you will have to calculate each cryptocurrency value to a single currency so you can compare apples to apples. An easy way to do this is to convert them all to a currency like the US dollar or the Euro. You can also convert them all to Bitcoin. So, if you have 1 BTC and 23 ETH in your portfolio right now and Ethereum price is 0.024 Bitcoin, then you can 'translate' your Ethereum into Bitcoin and you would have 0.552 Bitcoin in worth of Ethereum in your portfolio. In percentages, you would have 64.5% in BTC and 35.5% in ETH in your portfolio. I recommend that you keep your portfolio in a spreadsheet, with the percentages updated. There is software that can do this for you as we talked about in chapter 5, but you can do it perfectly using just a spreadsheet. You don't have to update your percentages three times a day, once a week is more than enough, so it's not that much work. Every time you buy, sell or exchange one of your cryptocurrencies, you must update your portfolio

The first rule of portfolio management is that you should try not to invest in many projects at the same time. Each project you add to your portfolio represents a periodic task. In the end, each cryptocurrency has its own characteristics and behaves in a certain way. Some are more stable, others are in full development and their teams are constantly launching new stuff, others are more affected by other markets, etc... In the long run, knowing how a specific project behaves is important and if you are investing in 50 markets at the same time you will not be able to know them well. My recommendation is that, to start with, you should not invest in more than 5 cryptocurrencies. Probably starting with less than 5 is a good idea but it will depend on how long you have been in this world and your knowledge. With time and practice you will be able to increase this number if you wish, but everything at the right time.

The second rule for portfolio management is to keep your risk low. Keep in mind that even the most established cryptocurrencies have very volatile prices, so try to reduce your investment in less established cryptocurrencies as these are generally too risky. An easy way to define if a coin is more or less established is what we discussed in chapter 4: using the range of Coinmarketcap, Coingecko, or similar pages. An established coin will be at the top of the list. Most of your portfolio should be in these positions. That is more than 50%. At the time of writing this book, the most established coins are Bitcoin and Ethereum and so far it doesn't look like this will change in the near future. A part of your portfolio should be in medium positions. Let's say that approximately 30% can be invested in cryptocurrencies up to ranking number 25. Right now interesting projects in that range include EOS, Tezos, Monero, ChainLink, Cardano, Tron (check the lists again as this is very variable)... And finally, the remaining 20% can be invested in less established coins that are below position 25 in the ranking, ranging from 25 to 100. These percentages are not written in stone. It's just a generally valid way to start, but it will depend on your risk tolerance and your experience and knowledge of each project. You can simply start with a portfolio that holds only established coins. Or eliminate the less established 20% of coins and stay at 70% established and 30% medium risk coins. What I do not recommend is that you increase the percentage of higher-risk coins, which means that you should not go over 20% of your portfolio in these types of coins.

You have to understand that the percentages will vary as you buy, sell, and exchange cryptocurrencies, and depending on the market cycle in which we are, it is more beneficial to reduce the percentage of portfolio in established coins and increase the percentage of medium-risk projects. The definition of market cycles and these changes in strategy depending on the market cycle will be discussed in chapter 13.

There is a lot of content in this chapter but we have taken an important step in our strategy. We have already defined our operation size and we have enough knowledge to put buy and sell orders in our exchange markets. We also know the tools that will allow us to control the risk and more importantly our reptilian brain. If you are completely new to this, this could be a lot of information. Don't hesitate to go over the chapters that are not completely clear to you. If you still feel that you are not completely grasping a particular concept, look for more information on the Internet about it. In the next chapters we will uncover tools that will allow you to decide when and at what price to put your buying and selling orders, and we will give the final touches to our strategy.

Chapter 10

Moving Averages

The Moving Averages or simply MA are one of the most used indicators and for that same reason, they are generally quite reliable. Moving averages use price information from a number of periods. The number of periods can be configured. The MA will be represented in our graph as a line. It is important to understand that the MA will depend on the periodicity of our chart. If we have an MA of 21 periods and we are looking at the daily candlestick chart, it means that the MA is being calculated as the average of the price of the last 21 days. If we are looking at the weekly candlestick chart, the same MA is being calculated as the average of the price of the last 21 weeks. For the same reason if we want to see an equivalent MA of the 21 weeks on the daily candlestick chart, since a week is 7 days, we will have to display the 147 day MA (7 x 21).

The most commonly used MAs are 21, 50, 100, and 200. If you are working in TradingView, in the top menu you have an item called 'Indicators'. If you click on it, a search tool will appear. If you type in Moving Average the indicator will appear. Once selected, it will appear on your chart and you will be able to set the indicator period on the top left of the chart. If you are using other software this can vary a bit but generally they work in a very similar way. TradingView also provides an indicator where you can set multiple MAs, there is a Triple MA indicator and a Quadruple MA indicator at the time of writing this book. Set your 21, 50, 100, and 200 MAs on your chart, each with a different color. Practice putting in and taking out different MAs, move to a different periodicity, for example, weeks, and watch how the price interacts with the different MAs.

Now that we have the MAs set up in our chart, let's see what they are used for in technical analysis. The MAs often act as support and resistance. We have already seen the concept of support and resistance in chapter 8. When the price approaches one of the most used MA, these can act as support or resistance. The longer the period of the MA, the greater the force of the support or resistance it will exert on the price. Therefore a 200 day MA will have more strength than a 50 day MA. And a 200 week MA will be stronger than a 200 day MA. It is important that when analyzing charts we take into account all the factors we see in this book. When we are looking at a graph we can't just look at the MAs. We have to add what we have seen in Chapter 8 and also what we will see in the next chapters. The set of indicators, oscillators, trends, and supports will tell us a much more complete story than if we only look at one indicator. For example, imagine that following the indications in chapter 8 we have identified a resistance zone in the BTCUSD chart around $8,000 and that the BTC price is at around $7,000 in an uptrend. Now, looking at the 50, 100, and 200 day MAs on your chart, you see that both 100 and 200 day MAs are above $8,000 but falling and approaching the $8,000 level. What this does is reinforce the resistance we had identified at $8,000. We could say that it would be a double resistance. Does this mean that it is impossible for the price to go above $8,000 in that case? No. Remember, we're always talking about possibilities. What it means is that the price, as it reaches that area, is likely to encounter more selling pressure, and therefore reduce its rate of rise — its momentum — and even begin to fall. We can think about MAs as moving supports and resistances, which can be added to the supports and resistances we identified in the price action, those explained in chapter 8.

In addition to acting as supports and resistances in a consistent way, we can use MAs to define a market trend very clearly. Many investors use the MA 200 daily to define whether we are in a bullish or a bearish market. If the price is above the daily MA 200, we are in a bull market. If it is below the MA 200 daily, we are in a bear market. A bullish market simply means that you are in a general uptrend, i.e. prices may go up or down today, but in the medium/long term they are going up. A bullish market can last from several months to several years. A bear market is the opposite, i.e. a market in which prices are falling in the medium/long term. The terms bull and bear have been traditionally used to define the market state. You will see the symbolism of bulls and bears all the time and everywhere. In fact, on Wall Street in Manhattan, you can find a very famous sculpture of a bull related to this market symbolism, but you probably knew that already. From now on we will also use these terms here to refer to the general trend of the market.

Using the 200 day MA or even the 250 day MA to define the general trend is a very simple and widely used form in traditional markets. But in the cryptocurrency market right now, in 2020, the price variations are higher than in the traditional stock markets so I recommend adjusting a little this rule to define trends. I consider that the 21 week MA is more adjusted to the cryptocurrency market right now and for the next years until it becomes a less volatile market. Remember that the 21 week MA is equivalent to the 147 day MA. So we will use this MA to define very simply whether we are in a bull market or a bear market. This is important because depending on what kind of market we are in we have to modify our buying and selling strategy. In a bull market, we will have more selling opportunities than buying opportunities. In a bear market, we will have more buying opportunities than selling opportunities, so your strategy should vary depending on the general market trend to be as efficient as possible and to keep a low-risk level. We'll look at these variations in much more detail in chapter 13 of the book, when we will have our strategy almost finished. For now, you have a simple way to identify the general trend of a market, and this will be an incredibly important tool for your strategy.

The truth is that sometimes it is not so simple to define a general trend and using only a simple indicator may seem simplistic but what we try to do here is to define a base strategy, as simple as possible, but valid initially, so that later this strategy can grow as your knowledge and experience grows. But even when your experience grows, I recommend that you keep the strategy as simple as possible when making modifications to it.

You can find a lot of information about moving averages and how to use them out there. You'll probably find terms like Death Cross or Golden Cross or exponential moving averages. Research, learn... that's always good, but for your initial strategy in investing in cryptocurrencies I think these concepts are not suitable because we try to create a really simple strategy. Nonetheless, I will still explain these concepts and why I would not include them in the initial strategy. The **Death Cross and Golden Cross** are based on 50 day and 200 day MA crosses. A Death Cross occurs when the 50 day MA crosses down through the 200 day MA. The general knowledge is that when a Death Cross occurs it means that the market will be down for a considerable time. A Golden Cross is the opposite situation, the 50 day MA crossing above the 200 day MA. When a Golden Cross occurs it is considered that the market will be up for a considerable time. These are indicators that have been used in traditional markets for many years to identify upward and downward trends. In my opinion, I believe that in the cryptocurrency market, where prices can vary sharply, golden crosses and death crosses do not have as much meaning as in traditional markets. Furthermore, cryptocurrencies are a very young market, with less than a decade of history right now, and Death Cross and Golden Cross do not occur very often so we do not have much data on which to base our calculations of the probability of success of incorporating these events into our strategy. When a Death Cross occurs, we are probably already in a bear market because usually when this happens the market has been down for a while. It is for these reasons that I think it is convenient that you understand these concepts, but that you don't use them as a basis for your initial strategy for investing in cryptocurrencies. You can use them as a complement to confirm a trend if you want, although, in my opinion, it is not necessary and adds complexity to your initial strategy. This may change in the future, and maybe in a few years we can prove these events reliable, but right now relying on Death Cross and Golden Cross to create a strategy for trading cryptocurrencies represents a risk that in my opinion is too high. In the daily BTCUSD chart, we can see that there is a Golden Cross at the end of April 2019 and a Death Cross at the end of October 2019. The Death Cross and Golden Cross can also be found in other periodicities.

BTCUSD daily chart with 50 MA and 200 MA

You'll also see that there are people who use exponential moving averages. These moving averages are similar to simple moving averages, which are the ones we use in our strategy, but they give more importance to the most recent periods. A 50 day exponential moving average will give more importance in its calculation to the prices of the last week than to the prices of 4 weeks ago. In my opinion, it is better to start using simple moving averages because in general they are more used than exponential moving averages and that means they will act more as support and resistance so they are a little more valid for our initial strategy.

Before you go any further, you must perform a task in your list of cryptocurrencies to invest in. Remember that in chapter 4 you created that initial cryptocurrencies list, with your notes on why each project is interesting and why it has a future. This should be a short list, 10-20 projects at most. In chapter 8 we added information about prices, current trends, supports, and important resistances to each of the pairs on our list. This information should also be up-to-date. If it is not, update it right now. Now, you should re-analyze the charts of each of the pairs with the information of the most used MAs. You should note if the price is near any important MA. For example, if you see that for a certain pair the price is in a downtrend, i.e. it is marking lower prices, but there is an important MA nearby that acts as a support, such as the 200 day MA, this is a pair you should watch more often as you might have a chance to buy in the next few days. You should also clearly note for each pair if we are in a bear market or in a bull market, and also, if we are approaching a possible cycle change. This is very important as our strategy will depend on whether we are in a bull market or a bear market. In this chapter, we have decided that we will use the 21 week MA to define the general trend of the market, bull market or bear market. So for each pair on your list, open the weekly candlestick chart and set the 21 MA on it. We will say that a pair is in a bull market when the **closing price** of a candle is above the 21 week MA. The pair will be in the bear market when the **closing price** is below this same MA. Most pairs will clearly be in a bull market or a bear market, but there will be situations where the price will be very close to the 21 week MA. Remember that we are analyzing weekly candles, meaning that each candle we see on the chart takes 7 days to close. This is important for you to understand. Remember how candlestick charts work. The closing price will be the top or bottom end of the candle body, depending on the color of the candle. If it is a rising candle, in green or another light color, the closing price is marked by the top of the body of the candle. If it is a descending candle, red, the closing price will be the bottom of the body of the candle.

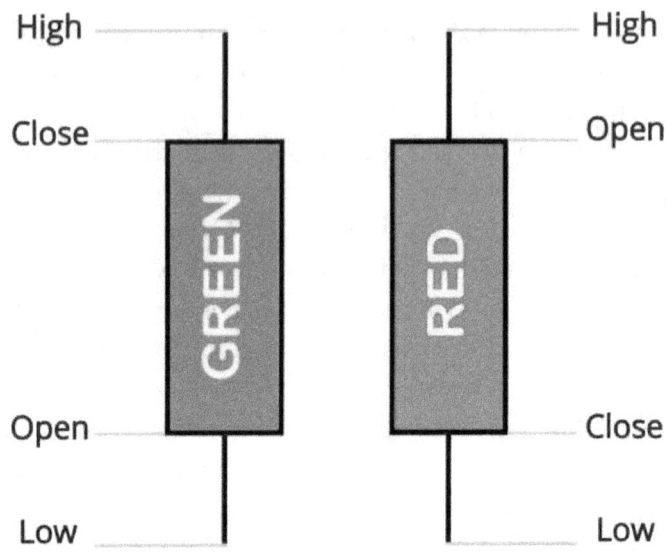

We will look at the closing price of the weekly candles to determine a general trend

We will run into situations where the MA is crossing the price candle. In that case, we cannot look at the last candle on the chart (the rightmost candle) because that candle has not yet closed, so we have to look at the previous week's candle, i.e. the second candle starting to count from the right. In the following image, we see part of the weekly candlestick chart for the BTCUSD pair from the spring of 2019. In this chart, we can see how during the week of March 18th, 2019, the price encountered resistance at the 21 week MA. The following week, the week of March 25th, the price crossed above the MA 21. From our point of view, the BTCUSD pair did not enter a bull market until the end of the week of March 25th and the beginning of the week of April 1st.

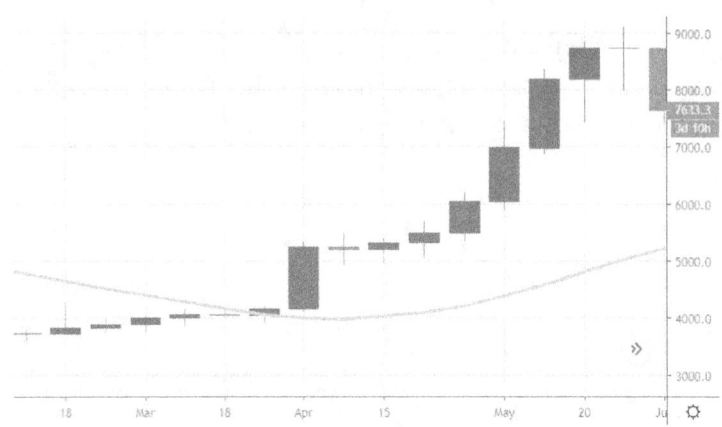

Weekly candlestick chart with MA 21

This is incredibly simple and fast to do. We have chosen this method to identify general trends because of its incredible simplicity and clarity. In our strategy, we will have no doubts about whether we are in a bull market or in a bear market. Update your list with this information.

So far we have seen different tools to identify areas where prices will slow down and even change direction. These areas are called supports and resistances. We've also learned to use a simple indicator to identify general market trends. Only with this, we could already define very simple strategies for long-term investors. For example, we could define a strategy where we buy when the price crosses above the 21 week MA and sell when the price crosses below the 21 week MA. This would be a strategy where we would not make too many trades. This is a completely valid strategy, but in this book, we will try to define a more efficient strategy. We will try to use the market movements a little more. To do this we can use other very handy indicators, called oscillators, to decide when to buy and when to sell. In the next chapter you will learn about the fascinating world of oscillators, simple tools to define entry and exit areas, i.e. buy and sell. I'll be waiting for you there!

Chapter 11

Oscilators

As you saw in the previous chapter, the MA are indicators that are drawn on top of the price chart. This is because they are used to identify crosses with the same price chart. Oscillators are indicators that are drawn separately. They have their drawing area separate from the price chart because they do not interact directly with the price. The indicators we have seen in the previous chapter are used basically to identify trends, that is, to identify in which direction the price is moving, up, down, or sideways. In contrast, the oscillators we will see in this chapter are another type of indicator: they are used to identify the force of a movement. The force at each moment will be indicated by a number from 0 to 100 and we will see how the oscillator creates a line that oscillates between 0 and 100, that's why they are called oscillators. Like trend indicators, or any other type, there are many of them that you can try with the click of a button in your charting system such as TradingView, GoCharting, or any other. For our strategy, and in my opinion, for any other valid strategy, it is important that we keep it simple, so here I will only explain some very basic oscillators that we will use in our strategy. I invite you to investigate on your own once you have more experience and master your base strategy to evolve it, but always remember that a strategy must be simple, that means that you should never use more than three indicators for the base of your strategy and you should always try to mix different types of indicators, for example, trend indicators and momentum indicators. If you use too many indicators in your base strategy, they will simply give you contradictory signals or similar signals that will make your decisions more complicated, besides, each type of indicator is more adapted to one trading style. For example, as a rule, trend indicators are better suited to investors. Oscillators tend to change more quickly and therefore are better suited to more active traders, such as swing traders or day traders.

The first oscillator we will see is the **RSI** and it is one of the most used. RSI stands for **Relative Strength Index**. It measures the strength of recent price changes. In this case we use 14 periods for the calculation, which in a daily chart would be the previous 14 days. The RSI is used to identify overbought or oversold moments. The picture shows a daily price chart for the ETHUSD with the RSI oscillator at the bottom. Open this chart in your charting system, and move to the first four months of 2020.

Price chart (above) and RSI (below)

In the picture, we can see how the RSI moves more or less like the price but within the range of 0 to 100. When the RSI falls from a certain level, usually 20 or 30, we say that the pair is oversold, that is, it is reaching the limit of its selling strength. On the daily chart, we can see a clear indication that the RSI has reached the oversold territory on the ETHUSD pair. When the RSI rises above a certain level, usually 70 or 80, it means that the pair is overbought, i.e. it is reaching the limit of its buying power. On the chart, we can see an overbought situation around mid-February 2020 for the ETHUSD pair.

As you have probably already deduced, if we wanted to design a strategy using only the RSI, we would buy during oversold situations (RSI less than 30 or 20) and sell during overbought situations (RSI greater than 70 or 80). These thresholds vary depending on the pair and the general trend you are in. For example, during a bear market, we will find more oversold situations than overbought ones. In the previous chart we see that we are in a bear market. Conversely, in a bull market, we will see more overbought situations than oversold ones, therefore we should adjust these thresholds to make our strategy as efficient as possible. Does this mean that whenever the RSI is telling us that a pair is oversold, the price will always go up? No. Remember this: There is no such thing as a perfect indicator. No single indicator will work for you in every situation, and therefore no single strategy will work for you in every situation. In the same chart of the image, you can see that after the first oversold situation the price keeps falling. There are always going to be situations where the indicators, and therefore the strategy, fails and that is why our strategy includes a series of risk control elements, which we have already discussed in previous chapters, such as controlling the order size and setting up stop loss orders.

In the strategy we are designing we will use a hybrid and different approach for each market trend, but it is important that you understand well how the RSI works since it is one of the most used indicators not only in cryptocurrency trading but in general. Now open your charting software and look for the RSI in the indicators menu. You may find it only by the acronym or by its full name: Relative Strength Index. In the case of TradingView it is the full name. Once the indicator is loaded, make sure it uses 14 periods for the calculation, otherwise you can use the configuration option to change it. We can also vary this setting depending on the pair or market trend to adjust it to specific characteristics but generally a period of 14, which is the standard, will work for you. That's it! It's as simple as that. You can now identify overbought and oversold situations.

Another commonly used oscillator is the **Stochastic RSI**. The Stochastic RSI uses the RSI values to perform its calculations. We could say that it is an indicator of an indicator. Like the RSI, the Stochastic RSI is an oscillator. Its value varies between 0 and 100 (or between 0 and 1 in some charting systems but it is equivalent). The Stochastic RSI simply tells us when the RSI has reached its high or low for a given period, usually the previous 14 periods calculated by the RSI. You do not need to understand how these calculations are made. What you need to know is that the Stochastic RSI fluctuates much faster than the RSI. It will go from 0 to 100 and from 100 to 0 many more times than the RSI, so the Stochastic RSI can be used for strategies or situations where you need to have more signals in a certain period of time. Since our strategy is a hybrid one, we will use the Stochastic RSI in different situations. Look for the Stochastic RSI in the indicator menu of your charting system and load it together with the RSI you already have loaded. Make sure that the Stochastic RSI is using 14 periods of the RSI. In the picture below we can see the ETHUSD daily chart with both oscillators activated.

From top to bottom: Price chart, RSI and Stochastic RSI

The first thing you will see is that the Stochastic RSI has two lines, usually a blue and a red one, although these colors may be different depending on your charting software — I have sometimes seen a white line and a red line — but they are equivalent. You should always look at the blue line or the clear line in case there is no blue line. One way to use the Stochastic RSI is to look for these two lines crossing, either up or down. The Stochastic RSI will also indicate overbought and pversold situations, but it will typically indicate more situations than the RSI in the same period of time. When the blue line is above 80, that's an overbought situation and below 20 it is an oversold situation. Since these two indicators work at different speeds, we will use them in our strategy for different market situations. We will see all this in chapter 13 where we will combine all this tools to define our buy and sell strategy.

As you can see from the charts, in a way, the RSI and Stochastic RSI follow the price movement. We can see how when the price forms a peak, the RSI does it too. We can also see that when the price is rising, the Stochastic RSI is also rising and vice versa. But there are some moments when this is not the case. We can find some situations when the price is marking a higher high than the previous one, but the RSI is marking a lower value than the previous one. The same thing can be found with the Stochastic RSI and the price. These differences between the behavior of the oscillators and the price are called **divergences** and are a quite powerful tool. They usually indicate a change in the price trend. If we see that the price is marking new highs, it means that the price is in an uptrend. But, if at the same time, we see that the RSI is making lower highs, it means that the RSI has initiated a downtrend. Usually, this means that there is a higher probability that the price will change direction, in this case, it will go from an uptrend to a downtrend. When we identify a divergence, we must take it into account for our strategic decisions. Open the daily BTCUSD chart in TradingView and view the period between August 2019 and March 2020. Add the RSI to the chart if you don't have it already activated. You should see a similar chart to the one in the image below, where I have marked two divergences between the price and the RSI with slanted lines.

Price and RSI divergence in BTCUSD daily chart

There's another very clear divergence in this chart that I haven't marked on purpose so you can find it. Can you find it? As you can see, some divergences last longer than others, generally a divergence in favor of the general trend has more strength so it will last less time. Divergences have a high probability, but like everything in this world of technical analysis, they are not infallible. You should always use them with the risk control tools you have learned in previous chapters.

Chapter 12

Other Techniques, Fibonacci and Figures

In chapters 10 and 11 we have discussed a few indicators. There are many more. If you have done a little research on your own, you have surely heard of many well-known indicators such as MACD, OBV, MFL, Bollinger Bands... There are countless indicators with their small variations and each one can have its use. There are also different drawing tools in the charts, there is a whole world of figures that are interpreted, ascending triangles, flags, Elliott waves... the range is immense. But we would need thousands and thousands of pages to explain them here. The purpose of this book is to help you define a trading strategy as simple as possible that does not consume too much time from your week and give you the indications for the strategy to be successful. I think that only using the indicators explained in the previous chapters is enough to design such a strategy. Combining indicators for a trading strategy, especially if the indicators are of different types can be very beneficial. But I don't think you should ever design a strategy that combines many indicators. Keep your strategy simple, three indicators is more than enough.

But it is also true that sometimes we can use some other tools besides our basic indicators to extract a little more information from the charts. The tools I will discuss here add complexity to our trading decisions so you should not include them in your initial strategy. I put them here as an extra content, and because I consider that once your strategy is designed it is important that you continue learning and evolving as a trader. You can never learn too much, but these tools will not be needed in your initial strategy. It is not recommended that you use these tools until you have perfectly mastered the basic strategy because they would add complexity to your strategy. Remember that simplicity is a key point of our strategy.

One such technique is Fibonacci. I'm not going to explain where the series of numbers comes from as this is fully documented and you can access this information easily on the Internet. Here I will just briefly explain how you can use this tool. Fibonacci levels will help you identify areas of support and resistance especially when the price moves against the general trend. As explained above the price action does not follow straight lines, it will move like waves, going up and then down a bit, then continue a bit further upwards. When the price is moving against the general trend for a while, it's called a retracement. Well, we can use Fibonacci to identify areas where these retracements could stop. Fibonacci is based on proportions found in nature and it is believed that human psychology also contains these proportions and that is reflected in the price movements because humans are buying and selling. I personally believe that it is more influenced by the fact that it is a tool that many traders use and the simple fact that many traders use it makes it have some chance of success. Be that as it may, it has a considerable probability of success if used well. To use it we need to be in a retracement already, and what we will do is use the 'Fibonacci Retracement' tool in our charting software. In TradingView this tool can be found in the left side menu under one of the options and is called 'Fib Retracement'. In GoCharting it can be found in the top menu, in the Drawing section and subsection 'Sacred Geometry'. Once you have selected the tool you will have to click on the start of the last movement in the direction of the general trend. If the general trend is downwards, the start of the last movement will be the crest of the last wave. If the trend is upwards, the start of the last movement will be the last low in the price. Once you have selected the beginning of the last move in favor of the trend you must select the end of that same move, right where the retreat begins. At that moment the tool will mark levels on the same chart: 23.6% retracement, 38.2% retracement, 50.0% retracement, 61.8% retracement... In theory, the retracement will be more likely to reach the intermediate points, which are 38.2%, 50% or 61.8%. My recommendation is that you don't use this tool alone. You can use it as a complement to make low-level decisions within your base strategy, but never as a base indicator. You can use the Fibonacci levels to reinforce support or resistance levels that you have already identified. Imagine that when you draw the Fibonacci Retracement, you see that the 61.8% level corresponds with the 100 day MA, then you can consider the support or resistance of the 100 day MA more important because the Fibonacci level coincides with this level. The Fibonacci tool is not necessary for the strategy we are designing in this book, but it is interesting to explore other tools so that you can use them in the future as a complement to your strategy for low-level decisions.

You may also have heard of chart patterns. There are a huge number of patterns: triangles, head and shoulders, cup and handle, ascending and descending flags... You can find a lot of information about each pattern on the Internet and other sources of information. My personal opinion is that these patterns are often very subjective. The human mind has evolved to identify patterns, especially visual ones, and for that very reason, you can find patterns everywhere in the charts. Have you ever played at looking for shapes of known objects in the clouds? In my opinion, patterns are much more subjective than indicators and therefore add a factor of doubt. That's why I don't recommend them for designing a strategy, let alone a strategy for someone who is just starting out in trading. In case you want to explore the world of price pattern trading, out of curiosity or to expand your tools, I wouldn't recommend you to mix indicators and patterns in the same strategy. For the same reason, I recommend that you don't mix many indicators in the same strategy; apart from adding a lot of complexity to your strategy you would get contradictory signals and create confusion, and there is nothing worse than having doubts at the moment of trading. If you are going to trade based on patterns you will need to learn very well how to trade each of the patterns, and only trade when the pattern has been confirmed (this is extremely important!). You also have to take into account when a forming pattern becomes invalidated... If you want to enter that world it is going to require considerable time and effort. This is my personal opinion and recommendation. Having said that, I also believe that the trader's journey is long and full of possibilities and each one must explore for himself and gradually define how to use each tool and how to integrate it into a strategy that makes sense for each type of trader and for one's personality and personal circumstances, but this only comes with experience and practice. For now, I recommend that you keep things very simple and use only the tools and techniques that you know well.

13

Strategy in Different Market Cycles

In this chapter, we will finish defining our trading strategy. We finally have all the tools and knowledge we need. That wasn't so hard, was it? This is going to be an intense chapter, packed with information. But before we start we're going to do a little review of what we've accomplished so far.

First and foremost, believe me, is to control your emotions. This is going to take some time, so we're designing a custom strategy to help you control your reptilian brain. It's no use having the best strategy for you if you don't follow it at the moment of truth, and I assure you that your reptilian brain will try to stop you from following it. Read chapter six again as many times as you need to. We have defined in chapter 2 what kind of trader we want to be. This is the basis for being able to define a strategy. In Chapter 4 we have defined a list of cryptocurrencies we may be interested in. It is recommended that you have this list in a spreadsheet or word processing document as you should keep this list updated. Cryptocurrencies evolve, change, new projects appear and other cryptocurrencies disappear. Remember that this list should be short; you should not focus on too many cryptocurrencies.

Then we have learned to read the price charts and to identify supports, resistances, and trends. The task of identifying supports and resistances, maximums and minimums, and trends in different periods is something that has to be done continuously. The easier it is for you to identify these price zones, the better a trader you will be. I recommend that when you do this task you clean up your chart, which means that you shouldn't have any indicators or trend lines that bother you. Just you and the price chart. Charting software usually has a utility to hide all the indicators and drawings in the charts. Use it. Remember to keep it simple. Use daily charts to get started and switch to weekly charts to see long-term trends and supports/resistances. After that, we have seen the different order types and how we can use them, and above all, you have decided on a very important part of your strategy: The position size. Remember that this size must be small enough so that your reptilian brain does not take over. Even so, I assure you that at the moment of putting an order, your reptilian brain (greed) is going to try to make you ignore your own strategy and take bigger positions. Don't fall into the trap! The design of the strategy includes the probabilities of a losing trade. You need to accept that sometimes trades don't turn out as you had thought. This is part of the strategy, it's part of the trading. Nobody can get it right 100% of the time, not even 80%, so the strategy must include this fact and to do so we must control the risk of the trade. If you take positions of 50% of your portfolio, you are breaking the foundation of your strategy, assuming too much risk. You may succeed in a trade but in the long run, it is a mistake. Remember that everything is based on probabilities and the fact that we cannot guess what will happen in the future, no matter how many indicators we use. I have already said this and I will repeat it again in the book because it is the basis of everything. We have also learned how to use a tool to control risk in your trades called stop loss and we have made it very clear that you should use it in your strategy. When you enter a trade you should always control the risk in case things don't go well and stop losses orders are designed for this task.

In chapter 10, we have seen how the MA will help us to define and enhance areas of support and resistance and, more importantly for our strategy, how to know in a very simple way what's the general trend in a market, i.e. whether we are in a bull market or a bear market. All this information should be kept on file and up to date with your list of projects and currency pairs that we've built up since Chapter 4. Finally, in Chapter 11 we learned how to set up and use oscillators. Now you must gather all this knowledge to finish defining your initial strategy for trading cryptocurrencies. Let's get to it!

We have already commented several times that the cryptocurrency market is characterized by high volatility in general, that is, prices can move sharply in very short periods of time. When we find ourselves in a bull market, the general market trend will be upward and the price will be creating higher highs. But there will also be price corrections. Our strategy should allow us to take advantage of these upward movements that can last for weeks or even months. We already defined in the second chapter of this book what kind of trader we are defining this strategy for. We don't want to be trading daily, this would be too risky if we don't have much experience and would also take too much time. Therefore we should look for indicators - or a combination of them - that give us the approximate input frequency we are looking for in a bull market and that allow us to have open trades long enough to seek maximum profit without taking too much risk. Remember this: in a bull market we will have more opportunities to sell than to buy, so we will try to relax the entry rules - buying - and we will be more strict in our exit rules - selling.

But what about bear markets? In a bear market, the general price trend is downwards. In other words, the price tends to create lower lows. The most important difference between a bear market and a bull market is that in a bull market we trade in favor of the general trend, but in a bear market we will trade against the general trend. This makes it riskier to trade in a bear market. The force of a price drop in a bear market can be brutal, therefore our strategy must take into account that there is a higher risk when trading in a bear market. In a bear market, we will have more opportunities to enter - buy - than to exit - sell - therefore we will have to relax the exit rules, and tighten the entry rules. This means that we will generally close our trades sooner in a bear market because at any point we could have a sudden price movement to the downside.

For these reasons, our trading strategy will have two distinct parts. Bull market strategy and bear market strategy. In a bear market, we will trade more because we will not take as much risk and will exit the trades sooner. We will also set up tighter stop loss orders as there is a greater chance of a price drop. In a bear market, we will be closer to what is considered a swing trader. In a bull market, we will be trying to make longer trades as there is a greater chance of the price continuing to rise. We will relax our stop loss strategy and make them much more loose because even if the price has a significant drop there is more chance that it will continue its upward trend in the longer term. Remember, it's all about probabilities. We could go straight to the strategy rules, but I want to tell you the logic behind building a strategy because the goal of this book is that you learn how to build your own strategy and have the tools to evolve your strategy as you gain more experience or the market changes over the years. I prefer to teach you how to fish than to give you the fish. You will see how everything is based on finding a balance between risk and profit. With every trade you make, you must reduce the risk of loss without reducing too much the possibility of a good profit.

As you can imagine, we could use that simple way of identifying bull markets and bear markets that we defined in chapter 10, using the 21 week MA. Also, you've already marked on your project list which pairs are in a bear market and which pairs are in a bull market, and also which pairs are close to a possible cycle change, so this work is already done. Remember that to confirm a cycle change, at least one weekly candle must clearly close on the other side of the 21 week MA.

Your strategy will give you signals to buy and sell. But the most important part of your strategy is not the one that gives you the signals, but the one that allows you to control the risk. Remember that every strategy will give you wrong signals at some point. Your strategy may give you several wrong signals in a row, so the most important thing is to keep the position size that we defined in chapter 9 and to put stop loss orders to limit the loss in case of a wrong trade. Let's define the buy and sell strategy in the different market cycles:

BULL MARKET STRATEGY

In a bull market, we want to make longer trades to let the price go up and thus increase our chances of making a bigger profit.

Remember that this market is highly volatile, therefore even in a bull market, we can have quite significant price drops without entering a bear market. But the chances of the price going up are also higher. Immediately after entering a trade – buying – we have to put a stop loss trade. This is not optional. The stop loss is what will reduce your losses and what will allow you to make a profit even with a high percentage of wrong trades. Later we will see at what price we put the stop loss, but first, we will talk about entry signals, or what is the same, buy signals.

BULL MARKET ENTRY

As we have deduced before, in a bull market we are going to find fewer occasions to buy at a good price, because the price tends to go down less than in a bear market, therefore we must relax the entry rules in order to not lose valuable opportunities. At the same time, we don't want to make too many trades and we want to leave room for the price to have its oscillations and continue to grow. Therefore in a bull market, we will use an indicator that marks a pronounced uptrend within the bull market. As you saw in chapter 10, MA's are very valid trend indicators, so we will use a tight MA for this: the 21 day MA. We will use the price cross with the MA 21, but combined with the RSI to detect oversold situations, where we will find the biggest profit. Therefore the rules for entering a trade in a bull market are:

1. Buy when the bull market starts if you don't have an open position yet. It is possible that coming from a bear market you already have an open position at the time the bull market starts. If you do, keep it open and use the bull market exit rules below. If you don't, you should find a

good time to enter. In this case, don't be too hasty as many times when we start a bull market the price can go back to the bear market zone in a few days. Remember that to enter a bull market the price must cross the 21 week MA. This weekly MA usually represents strong resistance, and many times the price will retest a strong resistance again once it is crossed, turning it into a support. Review chapter 8 if necessary to understand these typical price movements. And remember that from our strategy point of view we don't consider that we are in a bull market until at least one weekly candle has closed clearly above the 21 week MA, not before. If you rush in and enter earlier, you have a greater chance of getting into a bad trade.

2. Buy if the price is below the 21 day MA and at the same time the RSI is below 40 (relaxed oversold situation) and at the same time the Stochastic RSI has recently reached 0 or very close (<5) and it's rising again already. This means that the blue line has bottomed out and is heading up again, crossing above the red line of the Stochastic RSI. You may see the RSI reach 40 but the Stochastic has not yet reached the bottom. In that case, you should wait as it means that the downward price movement still has some force. Remember that the Stochastic RSI marks the strength of the movement, so in that case, there is a chance that the price will continue to fall. The RSI can sometimes reach very low levels in a bull market. The lower the RSI level, the better the buy, as it means we are in a deeper oversold situation. This means that if you see the RSI reaching 40 but still dropping, relax and watch the Stochastic RSI to know when to enter.

3. If the price is below the 21 day MA and the situation above

does not occur, but the price rises again above the 21 day MA, you should buy the moment the price crosses above the 21 day MA. This means that in our daily candlestick chart, there is at least one candle that closes clearly above the 21 day MA. Also, look at the Stochastic RSI to decide the exact moment to buy. If the Stochastic is dropping, take precautions and don't rush. Wait for it to move up again.

Remember that right after buying you should always put a stop loss to reduce the possibility of large losses. Also, once you have set these stop loss, you should immediately write down your trade in your history, adding your notes and all the information you think is necessary. In a bull market you must leave some freedom to the price to make its natural oscillations which, in the case of the cryptocurrency market right now, can be considerable. Let's see now how we can achieve that balance:

STOP LOSS IN A BULL MARKET

· You should put the stop loss at approximately 25% below the purchase price. This means you will be limiting your loss to 25% maximum. But this is 25% of your position size which, as we have repeatedly explained throughout the book, should be small. Therefore we are assuming a 25% risk on each trade. A 25% you may think is a high risk and in fact, it is, but this is because in the cryptocurrency market the price is very variable and movements of 25% are not uncommon when we are taking medium/long term positions like these. But this price variability is what allows us to aim for a larger profit. In our strategy, we will limit losses, but we will try not to limit gains. When you create a strategy your goal is to have a lower risk/reward ratio. This happens when the possibility of profit is higher than the risk you take. at least 2 or 3 times higher. Here we assume 25%, so our goal is to have a profit of at least 50% or 75%.

· You have to adjust the stop loss. The 25% that I have recommended in the previous point should serve as a guide, but at the time of putting the stop loss you always have to look at the different supports that are below the current price and the area around 25% below. This is when your notes will come in handy, since in your list of pairs to invest you should have written down the different supports and resistances of each pair. That's why it's important to have this list updated continuously. Let's take an example to make this clearer: let's say you just bought Ethereum at $192. Using the TradingView measurement tool (using the shift key and clicking on the chart) you calculate that 25% below the current price would be approximately $145. But it turns out that you have identified a strong support at $150. This means that if the price falls to these levels, it has a better chance of stopping and rising again to around $150 than around $145. In this case and since the support is very close to our calculated value for the stop loss it would be convenient to adjust the stop loss and put it just below the support we have identified so that in case the price reaches the support and rises again it won't trigger our stop loss order. We would put our stop loss order at the price of approximately $148. This means that we would have adjusted our stop loss to approximately -23%. If we found a support that is a little below our calculated point of 25% would be perfectly valid as well. Let's say you can adjust your stop loss point between 20% and 30% below the buy price depending on the supports you identify. Remember that MAs also form supports, but these supports are moving with time so they are less useful for adjusting stop loss orders.

BULL MARKET EXIT

Due to the bull market's history of incredible price increases, we should not limit the gains of our operations, for that very reason we will not place a sell order (or take profit order) immediately after entering the trade. To decide when to sell in a bull market we will again rely on indicators. In this way, we reduce the possibility of losses with our stop loss but we leave open the possibility of profits to take advantage of the volatility of the cryptocurrency market. Let's take a look at the exit rules in a bull market:

1. Sell if the RSI on the daily candlestick chart is clearly overbought, i.e. it is above 80 and at the same time, the Stochastic RSI has peaked (100 or almost 100) and is dropping. This means that the blue line on the Stochastic RSI has touched the top, and is already heading downwards having crossed the red line. Don't be too quick to sell in a bull market. You must follow the strategy but in a bull market a pair can be in an overbought state for several days, even weeks, and the RSI can continue to rise. The same goes for the Stochastic RSI. It can be in areas close to 100 and stay in those areas for many days and during those days the price can make significant gains, so if you see that the RSI has reached over 80 but at the same time you see that the Stochastic RSI is still strong, you should wait a while.

But you should always be vigilant in overbought situations as there is a good chance that the price is reaching a high and has a significant correction. So don't sell until you see that the Stochastic starts to fall, which means that the movement is losing strength. At that point, you must act quickly. As an optional and complementary method for overbought situations that last for several days in bull markets, what you can do is put a much tighter stop loss on the current price and move the stop loss as the price rises. This is called a trailing stop loss. A tight stop loss would be 7% or 8% below the current price.

2. If the situation described in point 1 does not occur and the price starts to fall, you should sell if the price crosses below the 21 day MA. Remember that for this to happen, at least one candle must close clearly below the 21 day MA. There are some situations in a bull market where the price drops for a few days below the 21 day MA and then rises again, as if the MA 21 acts as a spring. The third bull market entry rule of the strategy covers you in these situations. So when you sell because the price crossed below the 21 day MA, you should keep an eye on the price during the next few days as your strategy could flash a buying signal that will allow you to continue to take advantage of the price increase. Remember to always look at the direction of the Stochastic RSI.

It is possible that right after you exit your trade — after you sell —, the price will continue to rise. This will happen. It's impossible for a strategy to always give you selling signals at the price peaks. At that moment when you see that the price keeps going up, your reptilian brain will try to sabotage your strategy. But if your strategy doesn't give you an entry signal, you shouldn't buy again. If you fall into your reptilian brain's trap, that is, if greed can get the better of you, you will be risking the profits you have made so far, and what is worse, you will be giving your reptilian brain more power and missing an opportunity to learn how to control it. In these situations you must remember that you have made a successful trade, and that you have taken profits. There's nothing wrong with that. It's not about buying at the lowest point and selling at the highest, that's impossible. There is no strategy or professional analyst that can give you those buy and sell signals consistently. If that's your goal I can guarantee you'll lose your money. Your goal should be to sell at a higher price than you have bought. Plain and simple. You must set aside your ego and see the long-term value of a trading strategy that is protecting you from taking too much risk. If you cannot control your emotions, you will end up losing your money. This strategy is designed to make it as easy as possible to control your emotions, but you will still have to fight. Greed and fear will appear at key moments, I can assure you of that. You must be prepared and that is why I have repeated this so many times throughout the book. Controlling your reptilian brain is the key to any trading strategy.

BEAR MARKET STRATEGY

In a bear market, we will be trading against the trend and therefore we must be extremely cautious. We will have more opportunities to enter but we will also be faster to exit. We will use the Stochastic RSI more often as it is an oscillator that will give us more frequent signals by oscillating faster than the RSI and much faster than any trend indicator. At the same time, we should adjust our risk controls. The position size will be the same in both bull market and bear market, as we will have trades that start in a bear market and move to a bull market, i.e. we enter according to the rules of the bear market strategy, but for the exit, we will apply bull market's rules as the market will have changed its cycle.

EXIT IN A BEAR MARKET

1. If we have an open trade we must sell when we enter the bear market. Remember that we enter the bear market when at least one weekly candle closes clearly below the 21 week MA.

2. You should sell when the Stochastic RSI on the daily chart has reached 100 and is beginning to fall, that is, when the blue line has reached the top and then changed direction and started falling, crossing below the red line. This is a fairly strict exit rule. There will be situations where when you sell, the price keeps going up. Don't worry, in a bear market you will have more opportunities to buy. Control your greed in those moments and think that the strategy is designed to reduce the risk.

ENTRY IN BEAR MARKET

1. Buy when the Stochastic RSI on the daily chart reached 0 and starts to rise in the daily chart. Many times you will notice that the RSI on the daily chart is in the oversold region (RSI < 20). You don't have to wait until the RSI on

the daily chart is oversold to make a trade in a bear market, but if it does, it's a good idea to buy. Don't be too quick to buy during a bear market, remember that you will have plenty of opportunities to buy during a bear market. As always, you should watch out for nearby resistance zones before you buy. If you see a strong resistance zone above the current price, very close, it's worth waiting to see how the price reacts to that resistance. It is possible that in a bear market, the strategy gives you a buy signal when prices are falling sharply. At that point, your reptilian brain will try to control you. You will be afraid. But as always, you must control yourself and follow the strategy. If the price continues to fall, your strategy will prevent large losses. That's why we've designed a tighter risk control on the bear markets. You must be mentally prepared for failed trades. That way you will be able to overcome your fear and trade at a significant profit even in bear markets. Remember that just after buying you should always place a stop loss order.

STOP LOSS IN BEAR MARKET

- We have already commented that in a bear market we must extreme the risk controls. Given the fact that we have a stricter exit strategy in a bear market, we must also adjust our stop loss. When we trade during a bear market, we should put our stop loss 10% below the purchase price. You should adjust the stop loss if there is any strong support near the purchase price, but in a bear market, you should never put a stop loss lower than 12% below the purchase price. You should be more strict when adjusting stop loss orders in a bear market.

As you can see, this is a very simple strategy. You will only need to have the MA 21, the RSI and the Stochastic RSI on your charts. And basically, you will move between the weekly and daily periodicities in the charts. You can also visit the monthly periodicity from time to time to identify support and resistance areas and very long term trends. This simplicity will make you focus on price and trend, and not occupy your mind with a bunch of indicators, figures, and patterns. It will also allow you to analyze and make decisions very quickly, freeing up your time to do what you want. Remember that you should also use the 50, 100, and 200 MA to analyze the market and find supports and resistances. This will support your strategy. Keep your strategy simple. You should always exercise risk control, and above all, control your reptilian brain.

Some trading markets allow short trading or opening short positions. When you open short positions you can make money when the price drops. These trades are more complex and require you to "borrow" an asset while keeping the trade open. This means that there is usually a cost to keep the trade open and that you are trading with money that is not yours. I believe that these types of trades involve too much risk and I do not recommend them at all unless you are a very experienced trader. I would never include shorts in a trading strategy for someone who is just starting out so we will not include them in this book and I strongly recommend you against shorting any cryptocurrency until you have a lot of experience trading, controlling the risk and controlling your emotions.

BITCOIN AS A MARKET LEADER

In the cryptocurrency market, Bitcoin acts as a leader most of the time. This may change in the future, but at the moment there are no signs that this will change in the near future. Alternative cryptocurrencies, or simply altcoins, are all non-Bitcoin cryptocurrencies. Remember that this is a very new market. Until well into 2017 Bitcoin accounted for over 95% of the total market capitalization. Since then, things have changed, but at the time of writing this book, in 2020, Bitcoin still represents more than 60% of the total cryptocurrency market capitalization. It's a very corelated market so when Bitcoin price moves, it moves the whole market with it. When Bitcoin moves, everything moves. If Bitcoin goes down in price, the altcoins will go down in price, many times more sharply. If Bitcoin goes up, the altcoins will generally go up too, many times more sharply (but not exactly at the same time). This will continue to be the case as long as Bitcoin represents such a large percentage of the market. This is important for you. It means that even if you don't have any open trades in Bitcoin, you should always monitor and analyze the Bitcoin charts because these charts will give you an overview of the state of the market. How can you use this knowledge to adjust your strategy? It's very simple. Generally, when the market is up, you want to diversify. We talked in chapters 4 and 9 about how to identify interesting projects to invest in and how to spread your portfolio among these projects to have a controlled risk. In upward trends you should keep your portfolio balanced as explained in Chapter 9, in the Portfolio Management section. Over time, your strategy will give you signals to buy different pairs of cryptocurrencies that you are watching. There will come a time when you will have open positions in several pairs. This is what is called a diversified portfolio. But when Bitcoin enters a bear market, the altcoins will also enter the bear market and your strategy will give you signals to sell. When you're in a bear market, you should exercise caution so you should increase the proportion of established coins in your portfolio, and reduce the percentage of not-so-established coins. This means that in bear markets you should focus on the cryptocurrencies that are highest in the Coinmarketcap or Coingecko ranking.

Congratulations! You've got your strategy! This chapter has been very intense and hopefully very interesting. Please read it again, take notes, make a schema or diagram of the strategy and add it to your notes. And remember that you shouldn't change your strategy just because you've had two losing trades in a row. The strategy includes these types of trades. Remember that it is a game of probabilities. If every time an operation fails you change the strategy, you are also changing these probabilities with potentially disastrous results. You would lose control. Therefore you should not change the strategy continuously. Your strategy can evolve as you gain experience and as your portfolio grows but this is a slow process, a journey that takes years.

Chapter 14

Final Notes

I hope you have noticed that in this book I have not only offered you a simple strategy to start trading in the cryptocurrency market, but we have been building this strategy together, step by step and from scratch. During the different tasks proposed in the book, you have had to put a lot of effort, you have had to do your part, but that makes you really understand how it works. You have understood how the frequency of operations you want to perform will determine the time you dedicate to investing, and this in turn will determine a lot of the strategy you define. You have also understood the basis of the cryptocurrency market and a key concept right now: its high price variability. This feature offers incredible profit potential but is a double-edged sword: it also increases the risk of loss considerably. That is why we have spent some time talking about risk control tools and techniques and have seen how to use them in a trading strategy. I hope you have understood the importance of this. You have also learned how to use the most basic and powerful indicators, but most importantly, you have learned how to include them in a trading strategy. There are indicators that give signals more often than others and this feature is key to using one or the other in your trading strategy. You have understood how to combine different indicators to adjust the entry or exit for a trade. And we have also made a small introduction to the different techniques and tools you will find on your way.

I could have just given you the strategy, but there is much more value in explaining how to build a strategy. Your strategy is alive. First you must learn to control your emotions, your reptilian brain, and we have designed together a strategy that will allow you to perform enough operations and with a size small enough to learn to control your emotions in record time. Without a goal and an adapted strategy you would lose a lot of time and money until you reach that point. But now you have these two things. Once you master your emotions and your initial strategy, you can start making modifications, evolving your strategy, but only at that point. Remember that the cryptocurrency market is a young market that is constantly evolving, and in a few years, it may be better to adjust this strategy for a market with less volatility, i.e. a market with less risk and lower profit potential per unit of time. It is also quite possible that you will evolve yourself over time as a trader and investor. You may find that you want to reduce the number of trades you make per year. When you make changes to your strategy, you will have plenty of data on your files. That's why it's so important and why I've been insisting throughout the book that you keep your lists and notes up to date. Keeping an updated list of projects and pairs is key. You will have your notes on what cycle they are in, whether they are near a cycle change or whether they are near an entry or exit signal. This will allow you to make an analysis of each pair in record time. You will only need a few minutes a day, and depending on the general market situation you may not need to do anything for many days. Keeping your trading history well detailed and always with notes and screenshots is also very important. This will allow you to review and correct errors, but it will also serve as a database for modifying your strategy if you wish to do so in the future. At that time you will have the tools and knowledge necessary to do so and you can always revisit this guide if you feel it is appropriate. For that reason, you have made the effort to understand and practice with all the tasks in this book. Knowledge and experience is something much more valuable than a strategy. As the famous Chinese proverb says: "Give a man a fish and you will feed him for a day, teach him to fish and you will feed him for the rest of his life".

You have reached the end of this guide. Congratulations! But this is only the end of the first step in your journey to learn how to invest in the cryptocurrency market. Now you must put your knowledge at work, be constant and strict, take notes, and above all, control your emotions at key moments. With what you know now, and only with a little perseverance and discipline I am sure you will manage to control your reptilian brain, get incredible gains, and most importantly, get to know yourself a little better.

About the Author

Since he was a little boy, Miquel Vidal has always been obsessed with understanding how things work, the more complex the better. Now, with a professional career in technology and teaching, Miquel Vidal is passionate about two very different fields: economics and the knowledge of how the human body works. His passion for economics awakened just after he was forced to emigrate from Spain because of the 2008 financial crisis. The need to understand what happened was what pushed him to investigate and study the complex world of economics, but that crisis also led him to live in different countries, as diverse as Ireland, the United States, or Colombia, and to work for a company in Silicon Valley. His passion for understanding how the human body works is much older and has always been driven by his desire to live, not only more but also better. It is evident that these two fields, of incredible importance to everyone, are, most of the time, left aside by basic education within today's society. Because of this, his goal is now to transmit in a practical, simple, and applicable way, his knowledge and experiences acquired in these fields, in order to improve the life and well-being of as many people as possible.